THE PENGUIN POETS

D 12

CONTEMPORARY VERSE

The Penguin Book of

CONTEMPORARY VERSE

SELECTED WITH AN
INTRODUCTION AND NOTES BY
Kenneth Allott

PENGUIN BOOKS

HARMONDSWORTH · MIDDLESEX

FIRST PUBLISHED 1950

TO

Raymond and Rosa W.

MADE AND PRINTED IN GREAT BRITAIN
FOR PENGUIN BOOKS LIMITED
BY THE WHITEFRIARS PRESS LIMITED

Contents

Introductory Note

I

THIS collection contains 127 poems. I should have liked to print twice as many. Had I been able to do so, I should have added only half-a-dozen names (including, certainly, those of Christopher Fry, Ronald Duncan and G. S. Fraser), but I should have given much fuller representation to some twenty of the sixty-one poets already included. Sixty-two writers were approached and only once was I refused permission to print. Miss Edith Sitwell, from whose work I had selected two 'late' pieces for inclusion ('Still Falls the Rain' and 'Anne Boleyn's Song'), felt unable to grant my request on the ground that this selection would not do her justice. As a result there is a gap, which I regret, in the representative nature of this collection.

The character of the anthology and the limits that I have proposed to myself may be indicated quite simply. It is a collection of English verse written between 1918 and 1948. This statement is not to be taken as accurate to the letter. There are a few pieces composed earlier than 1918 – pieces, for example, by Isaac Rosenberg and Edward Thomas – but even here the impact of the poems on readers came somewhat later. Again, I spoke above of English verse, not verse in English. This division between English and American poets cannot be anything but artificial when Dylan Thomas, say, is read in Greenwich Village and San Francisco, and Karl Shapiro in Hampstead and Birmingham, but it was made inevitable by the necessity of the collection's appearance in a single volume. Of course I have not been absolutely consistent. I have excluded neither the poems written by T. S. Eliot before he became a naturalized Englishman, nor those written by W. H. Auden after he settled in America. But I have been compelled for reasons of space and economy to exclude American poets whom I admire, such as Ezra Pound, John Crowe Ransom, E. E. Cummings, Allen Tate, Frederic Prokosch, etc. I have also had to keep out translations – with the single exception of Arthur Waley's renderings from the Chinese. For practical purposes, then, this is an anthology of the poetic work of the 'twenties, 'thirties and 'forties in England.

In choosing the poems and putting together the commentary I have chiefly had in mind two classes of readers: the large class for which poetry of any kind is only occasional reading; and the smaller one – it contains many students – already interested in contemporary poetry, but unable to buy and keep on buying the many books of verse published to-day. For the sake of these audiences I have made the commentary as full and informative as possible, and I have not minded very much my own grumble that the consequent elementary approach meant a commentary without tears and without teeth. The usual biographical facts are included, but I have often gone beyond this in supplying bibliographical information about a poet's publications, or in listing studies of his or her work. I think that most of the information given will be useful to some reader. I have also committed myself – for the most part I hope without offence – to saying how I felt about the work of particular artists. This is to run the risk of scathing comment from those who do not recognize the difficulty of giving a summary judgment on a writer in a few lines, or who deny the use of such judgments altogether.[1]

1. A peculiarly painful example of the ineptitude of summary judgments on modern poets by academic critics can be found in the last three chapters of *A Critical History of English Poetry* (1944) by Herbert J. C. Grierson and J. C. Smith. It comforts me to think that where I have believed myself to be most platitudinous I may be saying something that still needs to be said.

For the sake of the readers I particularly had in mind I thought the risk worth taking.

Sometimes my estimate of a poet's importance is suggested by the amount of his work I include. There is more work by Yeats, Eliot and Auden than by other writers, and this fact coincides with my opinion that these are the most important poets in my collection. But often this mechanical kind of estimate would be misleading because of two complicating factors at work. First, the sorting-out process of time has operated more on the 'twenties than the 'thirties, and more on the 'thirties than the 'forties, so that I have been less and less selective as I approached the present. Second, I have occasionally given a writer more space than my strict opinion of his merit would allow, because I think he has had less than his due of esteem in other anthologies or at the hands of the critics.

Finally, while for the most part I have aimed at printing what I consider to be good poems, I have included a few pieces either because they are typical of a particular time or temper, or because they appear to have exercised an influence, or because their authors have large and deserved reputations in other branches of literature. It would be invidious to particularize about this matter at any length, but examples of these three classes may be found in the work I have printed by Aldous Huxley, Charles Williams and Herbert Read respectively.

II

In spite of its length this is an introductory note rather than an introduction, because any real introduction to the poetry of the last thirty years would have to run to many thousand words. Such an essay would allow those qualifications of general statements, those reservations about particular judgments, without which the critical process can only be seen as a rather ham-handed 'roughing-in' of outlines. For this reason, and because of the humbling effect of reading other people's introductions,

I decided at first to say my say about individual authors (and, incidentally, about groups, movements, tendencies and so on) in the commentary; and to leave it at that. Since then, however, several readers of the anthology in manuscript have recommended the pulling together of what is said or implied at various points in the commentary by an explicit report on the poetic 'weather' of the three decades. I have attempted this task. It has not been performed to my own satisfaction, because I do not think the job can be done so briefly, but half a loaf may be better than no bread.

Fortunately there is no need to describe again the characteristic insipidities of the Georgian poets with their cult of respectability and their pastoral week-end England of trout streams, parish churches, cricket and R.S.P.C.A. collecting-boxes: their influence on later poets has been negligible. Equally 'the opposition', represented by *Wheels*, an anthology first issued in 1916, can be quickly passed over. Miss Sitwell was the presiding genius of these irritated replies to the tame volumes of *Georgian Poetry* edited by Edward Marsh. Although Wilfred Owen and other good poets contributed to *Wheels*, and many of the pieces printed there have a certain technical liveliness, on the whole the content of the poems is uninteresting. Imagism will hold us back a little longer.

In time the Imagist movement mainly lies outside the period covered by this collection, but its demand for hardness, clarity and precision in writing, its insistence on fidelity to appearances, and its rejection of what was called irrelevant subjective emotion had later effects which are demonstrable. The movement was certainly more American than English – Ezra Pound spoke of 'Amygism' because of Amy Lowell's enthusiasm – but it had powerful English supporters and adherents. T. E. Hulme, for example, who was killed in World War I, by his ideas exercised an important influence on Pound and Eliot, and Hulme's 'complete poetical works' – he was primarily a philosophical essayist–can be found in an appendix to his posthumous volume, *Speculations :* they consist of five Imagist fragments. Imagism can be traced directly in Eliot's 'Preludes' and in such pieces as 'Morning at the Window', and more indirectly in the kind of descriptive writing done by Pound in his 'Chinese' poems, by D. H. Lawrence in his animal and flower pieces, and by Richard Aldington in such a narrative as *A Dream in the Luxembourg.* The Imagist aims of precision and clarity of outline have also to be held in mind when we remember Pound's plea for the imitation of Gautier's *Émaux et Camées :* this plea fathered Eliot's 'Sweeney' poems in quatrains and Pound's own famous sequence *Mauberley.* Further, the rejection of conventional verse forms by many poets in the 'twenties owed something, I think, to the Imagist repudiation of flabby writing by the Georgians. Other reasons, of course, predisposed poets to the adoption of *vers libres*–the mere desire for novelty, the imitation of Whitman, the study of Jacobean dramatic blank verse, awareness of what French poets had already done to the alexandrine in France. It was difficult, to say the least, for a poet of the poetic generation of the 'twenties – the qualification is important – to handle a conventional verse form such as the sonnet or the heroic couplet with any vitality during these years. After their long misuse these patterns had to be rested before they could be employed to advantage again in the 'thirties and 'forties.

One way of looking at poetic periods is to notice what contemporary interests and knowledge penetrate the best verse written at the time, and what moods are permissible in treating of these matters. From this point of view T. S. Eliot must be saluted, however bookish and esoteric his early poetry may seem (up to and including *The Waste Land*), for his extension of the field of subject-matter available for poetic treatment. Christianity, the modern industrial city and the background of

European history are found a place in his poetry, as MacNeice has remarked, and wit, irony and satire are weapons at his command. To argue that this widening of subject-matter is in Eliot's favour is not to deny that particularly in lyric verse comparatively simple nature-poems or love-poems could be written successfully; but it is to suggest that good nature-poetry or love-poetry should reveal contemporaneity in some difference from earlier work in the same kind. In his choice of themes Edmund Blunden is a traditional poet, but especially by his use of rhythm and by word-selection he creates a subtle impression that he is aware of the artificiality of what he is doing, and this impression is a witness to his poetic integrity and to the responsibility of his verse.

If we speak of the 'twenties as being concerned in poetry with culture and the maintenance of tradition, we have to forget the puerility of much of the verse published in the *London Mercury*, the absurdity of the *avant-garde* chopped prose of Bloomsbury and Paris, and the dullness of the innumerable slim volumes of garnered fancies issued by publishers out of habit or in the whimsical hope of cornering a future best-seller novelist. We have to put aside, that is to say, a quantitative assessment in favour of a qualitative one. Qualitatively the poetic 'twenties may be said to have undertaken the defence of culture and tradition because T. S. Eliot, their arch-poet, did so. That defence meant an acquaintance with the English and European past, not only literary but religious and social. It meant, too, much critical activity in the attempt to understand and value the tradition. Eliot's critical work in prose accompanies his poetry with equal steps, and Miss Bradbrook has shown (*Focus* 3) the same preoccupations in each – the concern with 'metaphysical' wit, the rejection of the Miltonic sublime, etc. A poet educated to his finger-tips will tend to be allusive. The danger of this Atlas-load of the past to be carried by the contemporary poet if he is to size up his own time is, of course, the danger of smothering and losing the poetry, of its becoming clogged with erudition and complexity. At this moment (1921) Eliot saw no way out of the dilemma. He wrote:

> 'We can only say that it appears likely that poets in our civilisation, as it exists at present, must be *difficult*. Our civilisation comprehends great variety and complexity, and this variety and complexity, playing upon a refined sensibility, must produce various and complex results. The poet must become more and more comprehensive, more allusive, more indirect, in order to force, to dislocate if necessary, language into his meaning.'[1]

There is a real meaning to be given to these sentences, but it may be argued that *The Waste Land* (1922) is a triumph partly because of the genius of its author in finding a technique for suggesting so many things simultaneously and for operating on so many planes of meaning. It is a most extraordinary poem, and perhaps it has become so hackneyed to some of us that we fail to see how truly extraordinary it is. Perhaps it was the only kind of 'masterpiece' possible in 1922, but after the lapse of a quarter of a century I am not at all sure of the satisfactoriness of the kind. By the side of Eliot's magnificent *Four Quartets* it seems to me too clever and too full of tricks, serious enough but even serious in what is almost a pedantic way – a poem coral for *Scrutiny* reviewers to cut their milk-teeth on, a poem to end poems.

In 1932, ten years after the publication of *The Waste Land*, Dr F. R. Leavis brought out his *New Bearings in English Poetry*, an important book if we wish to discover the orthodox 'advanced' view of contemporary poetry held by an adult, purely critical intelligence at the beginning of the 'thirties.

1. Some of these 'dislocations': Joyce's polyglot word-coinages, the Stein stutter (to use Wyndham Lewis's phrase), the lingua franca of *Transition*.

New Bearings in English Poetry contains three long essays devoted to Gerard Manley Hopkins (first published in 1918), Ezra Pound and T. S. Eliot. The Pound of *Mauberley* was preferred to the Pound of the *Cantos* [1] – the Ezra Pound, that is, concerned like the Eliot of *The Waste Land* with the necessary health and actual sickness of our contemporary culture. To Eliot this was a matter of the community's loss of vitality and of a sense of purpose as a result of a decay in religious beliefs. Ezra Pound expressed more simply his hatred of drabness and levelling-down in a commercial and industrial society. Over a century ago Alexis de Tocqueville spoke of the apotheosis of the mediocre in a democratic community, and both Pound and Eliot show more than a normal distrust of democratic tendencies in politics because they approach the social problem too exclusively from the side of the maintenance of cultural standards. W. B. Yeats, it will be remembered, saw 'mere anarchy ... loosed upon the world' in the squeezing out of aristocrat and peasant by the time-ridden, gadget-employing middle class. But to none of these poets is man primarily a political animal with his natural habitat the hustings or the conspiratorial backroom of a shabby café in a dock area. It would be an exaggeration to say that the new poets of the 'thirties did hold this view, but such an exaggeration would underline correctly enough a basic difference between the poetry of the 'twenties and 'thirties.

In the last chapter of the book by Dr Leavis, mentioned above, two poets were briefly discussed and their verses singled out for praise as growing-points in any plausible future of poetry. The first of these poets was William Empson, who has a fine mind and is at times an exciting poet, but often expresses himself in words of nearly impenetrable obscurity; the second, whom Dr Leavis seemed to prefer, was Ronald Bottrall. Bottrall was so distinguished, it must be supposed, because his verse showed

1. The comparative failure of the *Cantos* reveals that T. S. Eliot made a correct decision in trying to 'write his epic small' in *The Waste Land*.

Mr Eliot's preoccupation with cultural standards, because it was educated and allusive. In fact at its worst it was simply Eliot pastiche. But by 1932 the time had gone by for a valuable development in poetry in imitation of T. S. Eliot. Political and economic forces at work in the world were compelling new poets whose eyes strayed from their books to see the cultural problem as one aspect of the general problem of the remaking of our society. *Transitional Poem* (1929) by Cecil Day Lewis had the usual *Waste Land* apparatus of notes containing references to Dante, Spinoza, Wyndham Lewis, etc., but Auden's *Poems* (1930), Spender's *Poems* (1932), and Day Lewis's *The Magnetic Mountain* (1933) revealed the new social attitude in various ways and upset Dr Leavis's predictions about the lines on which poetry was likely to develop. *The Magnetic Mountain* is too much a tract for the times at a journalistic level to be anything but a poetic failure *as a whole*, but a rather simple-minded fervour for a new world of political and economic justice is less evident in Auden and is more poetically conceived and felt by Spender – Auden from the beginning diluted his Marx with Freud, and in *The Destructive Element*, a book of prose criticism, Spender argued that a Marx-Freud marriage should be fruitful. The present point, however, is that all three poets – and others associated with them – would have accepted Michael Roberts's statement in his anthology *New Signatures* (1932), a statement obviously put together to counter Eliot's claim (already quoted) that poetry *must* be difficult in the complexities of the modern world.

'The solution of some too insistent problems may make it possible to write "popular" poetry again ... because the poet will find that he can best express his newly-found attitude in terms of a symbolism which happens to be of exceptionally wide validity ... The poems in this book represent a clear reaction against esoteric poetry in which it is necessary for the reader to catch each recondite allusion.' [1]

The most creative mind, the most original poetic force in the new movement of the 'thirties was W. H. Auden. Dr Johnson tells us that after Addison's *Spectator* papers on *Paradise Lost* most readers thought it 'necessary to be pleased' with Milton. Similarly in the 'thirties most young writers thought it necessary to be pleased with Auden, and a certain amount of social reference even in the personal lyric was the literary equivalent for a Party Card. The crudities of this view can be laughed at now, and, in the hands of poetasters, the results of it were often laughable then, but it is much harder to say that this insistence on social reference was a bad thing. The political aspect of the social attitude can be exaggerated. Auden spoke of a poet being 'a bit of a reporter' (not simply a *political* reporter). Geoffrey Grigson in the preface to his *New Verse* anthology (1939) revealed his method of assessing contemporary poems:

'I always judge poetry, first, by its relation to current speech, the language in which one is angry about Spain or in which one is pleasant or unpleasant to one's wife. I judge every poem written now, by poets under forty, by the degree to which it takes notice, for ends not purely individual, of the universe of objects and events.'

The phrase about Spain may seem significant, but in reality it is not much more than a hurried genuflection. Louis MacNeice, too, has something to say in 1938 about the qualities necessary for the ideal poet.

'My own prejudice ... is in favour of poets whose worlds are not too esoteric. I would have a poet able-bodied, fond of talking, a reader of the newspapers, capable of pity and

1. Louis MacNeice in *Modern Poetry* (1938) was the first, I think, to set this quotation against the earlier one from Eliot's essay on *The Metaphysical Poets* (1921)

laughter, informed in economics, appreciative of women, involved in personal relationships, actively interested in politics, susceptible to physical impressions.'

MacNeice obviously wants the poet to keep his eyes open – 'social reference' did not go beyond this in many poets of the 'thirties – and I suspect that 'informed in economics' and 'actively interested in politics' breathe temporary aspirations induced by the *Zeitgeist*, but never taken very seriously by MacNeice himself.

New Verse, the most important verse-magazine of the 'thirties, founded by Grigson in 1933, had no left-wing axes to grind and was often attacked by left-wing enthusiasts for its political irresponsibility, but a glance through a few old numbers will show more quickly than pages of comment what is meant by 'social reference'. Subject-matter is sometimes directly political, most frequently in Stephen Spender, but the social approach to 'experience' by poets is evident in a more general way in their attitude to the problem of communication. Auden and Spender are occasionally difficult in their early work (not always excusably), but one is aware of a concern for reaching a public, a care for intelligibility which prevents the more private extravagances found in the 'twenties. Behind the creation of light verse [1] (cf. Auden's ballads and the 'Letter to Lord Byron') and the wish to return to traditional forms such as the sonnet, the couplet; *terza rima*, the sestina; behind the move to employ new media – the sound strip of documentary films, the radio feature-programme – as behind the attempt to establish poetic drama, there lay an urge to proselytize. The poets wished to make contact with as wide an audience as

1. Auden's light verse expresses the normal Auden personality in a lighter mood; Eliot's light verse is a conscious unbending – the poet is going to play with the children, and he is aware that he has to get down to their level. This weakness – I believe it to be one – is analogous to that of T. S. Eliot's attempts at working-class colloquialisms. Cf. the pub cronies in *The Waste Land*, the unemployed in *The Rock*.

possible, and they had designs on their public, they wished to
teach it something. The 'social' poets had a reasonable hope that
what they had to say would be understood, because their view-
points, and the imagery used to illuminate them, were drawn
from a direct analysis of the contemporary world. Louis
MacNeice's way of putting this cannot be bettered:

> 'These new poets, in fact, were boiling down Eliot's
> "variety and complexity" and finding that it left them with
> certain comparatively clear-cut issues. Instead, therefore,
> of attempting an impressionist survey of the contemporary
> world – a world which impinges on one but which one
> cannot deal with, they were deliberately simplifying it,
> distorting it perhaps (as the man of action also has to dis-
> tort it) into a world where one gambles upon practical
> ideals, a world in which one takes sides. ... This does not
> mean, however, that their world is a crude world of black
> and white, of sheep and goats.' [1]

As a poetic personality MacNeice may be described as
l'homme moyen sensuel. Not much of his verse is political in any
sense – *Autumn Journal* is to some extent an exception – but the
above quotation and the earlier description of the ideal poet
(p. 20) give us an inkling of what his verse owes to the social
attitude of the 'thirties, and what it might have been without that
attitude and without Auden's direct influence. The difference
between MacNeice's volume of juvenilia, *Blind Fireworks* (with
its intelligent frivolousness and rather thin gaiety), and
Poems (1935) shows the kind of intellectual stiffening provided
for him by 'social reference'. The case of Cecil Day Lewis is
more doubtful. It has been said that he is really a Georgian in
temper and natural interests, and that his latest (and best) work
shows this bent clearly enough, but I think that in his non-
political poetry he writes better than most of the Georgians, and

1. *Modern Poetry*, pp. 15, 25.

I am inclined to attribute this to the existence of the special poetic character of the 'thirties.

We may sum up what has been said in the last few paragraphs about the social poetry of the 'thirties by a quotation from Stephen Spender. At that time, he writes:

> ' ... there was a group of poets who achieved a very wide reputation as a "school" of modern poetry. They were not in a deliberate sense a literary movement ... [but] they had certain ideas in common. They consciously attempted to be modern, choosing in their poems imagery selected from machinery, slums and the social conditions which surrounded them ... Their poetry emphasised the community, and, overwhelmed as it was by the sense of a communal disease, it searched for a communal cure in psychology and leftist politics. ... To a great extent, their poetry, though leftist, expresses the problem of the liberal divided between his individual development and his social conscience.' [1]

To turn to the 'forties and attempt to find a poetic character for them is first to observe that even in the previous decade there had been a reaction against poetry as 'social reporting' in favour of poetry as 'individual development' or 'self-unravelling'. This reaction is most noticeable in the work of Dylan Thomas and George Barker. If the social poets wished to marry Marx and Freud, Dylan Thomas may be said to have married the Old Testament and Freud, and his Freud is seen through D. H. Lawrence – no longer a scientist and intellectual, but a 'thinker with the blood'. George Barker is of particular interest here, because, possessing less self-assurance than Thomas, he hovered so uneasily between the two kinds of writing in the 'thirties, to the detriment, it must be said, of much of his verse. In 1939 a group of young writers called themselves the New Apocalypse and made the reaction overt. 'Their model for the writing of

1. *Poetry since 1939*, p. 28.

poetry was Dylan Thomas,' Julian Symons has remarked, 'and for many of their theories of art, as they have frequently acknowledged, they are indebted to the ideas of Herbert Read.' They rejected what they described as the self-conscious and intellectualized manner of Auden and his associates, preferring to become intoxicated with words, to create myths and to indulge in Gothic effects. The New Apocalypse included few good poets and its importance is mainly to point to changes taking place in the cultural weather. The Apocalyptics disliked the machine, flirted with anarchism, and would have agreed with the 'individualist' E. E. Cummings who wrote:

> 'dead every enormous piece
> of nonsense which itself must call
> a state submicroscopic is –
> compared with pitying terrible
> some alive individual'

The changes which were taking place in the cultural weather – they were to become more obvious during the war years and the years immediately following the war – were, like the changes heralding the social poetry of the 'thirties, not a mere literary fashion, but a reflection of forces in the actual world and the feelings of men and women about them. Militarism, bureaucracy, Russian foreign policy, the melted eyeballs of the Japanese at Hiroshima, weariness of slogans and propaganda lies, with a hundred other matters great and small, conspired to produce an atmosphere in which all political optimism and idealism seemed childish. E. M. Forster's novels were read with wide appreciation because Forster found bed-rock only in charity in personal relationships. Graham Greene was enjoyed and he had written of a journey to Africa:

> 'There are others who prefer to look a stage ahead, for whom Intourist provides cheap tickets into a plausible future, but my journey represented a distrust of any future based on what we are.'

There was an increased understanding and valuation of T. S. Eliot – the Eliot of *Four Quartets* – and a number of the younger poets found meaning and consolation in Christianity, were convinced like Newman of some 'aboriginal calamity' when they looked out on 'the disappointments of life, the defeat of good, the success of evil, physical pain, mental anguish, the prevalence and intensity of sin ... a vision to dizzy and appal.' The names of Anne Ridler, Kathleen Raine, Norman Nicholson and David Gascoyne come to mind. There was a neo-romanticism in poetry which bound together writers of widely different temperament and technical adequacy – Vernon Watkins, Sidney Keyes, John Heath-Stubbs, Laurie Lee.

Geoffrey Grigson has written harshly of neo-romanticism. In an essay, first published in *Polemic*, he says :

> 'The "romance" we are drifting back to is a romance without reason: it is altogether self-indulgent and liquescent. An Inky Cap mushroom grows up white and firm and then flops down into a mess of ink – which is our new romance ...'

Grigson may well be right in remarking that 'there is no body of opinion [in literature] about what is true and untrue, possible and impossible, probable and improbable.' The neo-romantic poets lack a sense of limit provided in the 'thirties by the concern with communication. They have poetic energy, but perhaps they are less aware than they should be of the need for organizing and directing it. There is a good deal of loose, obscure, slapdash verse-making in the 'forties, but it is impossible to indict a whole poetic decade, or even that part of it represented by the neo-romantic poets. I have said that Vernon Watkins can be described as a neo-romantic, and he can write with a fine, musical precision. Other poets have cultivated their hysteria and built themselves ivory towers. Their verse is either dark, prolix and unnecessarily involved – this is the commoner fault — or a lisping 'silly sooth'. Examples had better be suppressed. There is also this to be said: Dylan Thomas has in the 'forties come a long way from the riddling darkness of some of his earlier poems in the direction of greater discipline over his very considerable gifts, and in the direction of a continuous, rather than a spasmodic, attempt at narrative meaning.

It is interesting when we consider the new cultural weather of the 'forties to see what has happened to the poetry of the social poets, Auden, Spender and MacNeice. We find Auden moving — to borrow a phrase from Arthur Koestler — from the commissar to the yogi end of the spectrum: attempting in *For the Time Being* to understand the meaning of the Incarnation, expressing in *The Age of Anxiety* his sense of crisis and of an abandoned world. We find Spender in *Life and the Poet* unsaying what he said in his *Forward from Liberalism*, and in his 'Spiritual Explorations' exploring an intuitively-accepted ethical-humanist position. We find MacNeice in 'The Kingdom' asserting the worth of the individual in a way that reminds us strongly of E. M. Forster's ideas. Something more is said about these developments in the commentary, but the reader can get a rapid picture of the magnitude of the change by comparing a 'political' chorus from *The Dog Beneath the Skin* with Herod's speech in *For the Time Being* or Malin's final soliloquy in *The Age of Anxiety*. Some of the poets of the 'thirties have adopted a religious attitude in rejecting the adequacy of a social interpretation of reality: others go no further than Stephen Spender, who writes in *Life and the Poet*:

'The ultimate aim of politics is not politics, but the activities which can be practised within the political framework of the State. Therefore an effective statement of these activities — such as science, art, religion — is in itself a declaration of ultimate aims around which the political means will crystallise ... A society with no values outside

politics is a machine carrying its human cargo, with no
purpose in its institutions reflecting their cares, eternal
aspirations, loneliness, need for love.'

This seems to me true. Unfortunately it is also true that this
scrupulosity about the nature of the social responsibility of
artists can serve as an argument for mere social irresponsibility,
can be used to support verse which is again private (as a padded
cell is private), vague and rhapsodical. The younger poets do
well, I think, to resent the way the importance of the free
individual is lessened in our mechanized and regimented 'great
society', but they should remember, in Auden's words, that
there are *two* lies:

> 'The romantic lie in the brain
> Of the sensual man-in-the-street
> And the lie of Authority
> Whose buildings grope the sky:
> There is no such thing as the State
> And no one exists alone;
> Hunger allows no choice
> To the citizen or the police;
> We must love one another or die.'

                                                K. A.

December 1948

W. B. YEATS

W. B. Yeats was born at Sandymount in Ireland in 1865 and educated at schools in Hammersmith and Dublin. He studied art for three years before turning to literature, and his first volume of poems was The Wanderings of Oisin *(1889). With Lady Gregory and others he helped to establish the Irish National Theatre in 1899. From 1922 to 1928 he was a Senator of the Irish Free State, and in 1923 he was awarded the Nobel Prize for Literature. He died at Cap Martin in the south of France in January 1939, and was buried in the cemetery of Roquebrune. He had been busy correcting his last poems to within forty-eight hours of his death – there is an account of these last days in* Letters on Poetry from W. B. Yeats to Dorothy Wellesley *(1940). His body was brought back to Ireland in September 1948, for reburial, this task being – Yeats would have appreciated it – the first expedition of the Irish Navy outside territorial waters.*

In a short note it is impossible to mention even the main events and interests of Yeats's life, or to give anything like a list of his publications. These can be found in the many biographies and critical studies, among the most useful of which are: The Poetry of W. B. Yeats *(1941) by Louis MacNeice,* The Development of Yeats *(1942) by V. K. Narayan Menon, J. M. Hone's* W. B. Yeats 1865–1939 *(1942) and* W. B. Yeats *(1949) by A. N. Jeffares. The following books by Yeats may be recorded:* Collected Poems *(1936),* Last Poems *(1939),* Collected Plays *(1934),* Autobiographies *(1926),* A Vision *(1937) – the last of importance for the poet's ideas of magic.*

Verses on the death of Yeats were written by Auden (v. Another Time*), George Barker (v.* Lament and Triumph*) and the present writer (v.* The Ventriloquist's Doll *and p. 208 of this anthology). The first poem of* The Lamp and the Veil *by Vernon Watkins describes a visit to Yeats in a very, perhaps too, successful imitation of his style.*

'*I had learned to think in the midst of the last phase of Pre-Raphaelitism,*' Yeats tells us. *His poetic development is from romantic themes carried by hypnotic rhythms and a Yellow Book diction – 'Innisfree' is dated 1893 – to the treatment of any and every theme in active, wideawake rhythms and a diction perpetually refreshed by contact with common speech. He did not come to love the actual, if by the actual we mean the modern scientific, commercial, middle-class world, but he came to face it and to oppose to it the ideal of an improbable aristocracy. The change in the poetry of Yeats is gradual and continuous, but it is first strikingly evident in the poems published in* The Green Helmet (*1912*).

'*How small a fragment of our own nature can be brought to perfect expression, nor that even but with great toil, in a much divided civilisation,*' *says Yeats in the* Autobiographies. *This insight defines not only his own problem but the problem facing most contemporary poets, and the measure of his greatness as a writer is his success in stating the difficulty and the integrity with which he worked for its solution.*

The earliest of the poems printed here is 'A Song', which comes from The Wild Swans at Coole (*1919*). *Like 'Long-legged Fly' from* Last Poems (*1939*), *it illustrates the superb use made of the refrain by Yeats. 'A Prayer for my Daughter' from* Michael Robartes and the Dancer (*1921*) *is included as an example of his mastery of recalcitrant material – the reflections are given lyrical intensity by Yeats's passion for his near-tragic view of life and by his use of reference and symbol. 'Leda and the Swan' is from* The Tower (*1928*) *and 'Byzantium' from* The Winding Stair (*1933*). *The latter poem should be read in conjunction with 'Sailing to Byzantium'* (The Tower). *'Sailing to Byzantium' contrasts the ephemerality of man with the permanence of art, represented there by the golden bird – 'I have read somewhere that in the Emperor's palace at Byzantium was a tree made of gold and silver, and artificial birds that sang.' For a discussion of the genesis and meaning of 'Byzantium' see an article in the* Review of English Studies (*Vol. 22, 1946: No. 85*) *by A. N. Jeffares.*

'*The Circus Animals' Desertion' from* Last Poems *is a poem about not being able to write a poem. Yeats rehearses the themes of*

*his earlier work and relates his myths and symbols to his own
life and needs, but he knows that*

> *'Players and painted stage took all my love
>   And not those things that they were emblems of.'*

A Prayer for My Daughter

Once more the storm is howling, and half hid
Under this cradle-hood and coverlid
My child sleeps on. There is no obstacle
But Gregory's wood and one bare hill
Whereby the haystack and roof-levelling wind,
Bred on the Atlantic, can be stayed;
And for an hour I have walked and prayed
Because of the great gloom that is in my mind.

I have walked and prayed for this young child an hour
And heard the sea-wind scream upon the tower,
And under the arches of the bridge, and scream
In the elms above the flooded stream;
Imagining in excited reverie
That the future years had come,
Dancing to a frenzied drum,
Out of the murderous innocence of the sea.

May she be granted beauty and yet not
Beauty to make a stranger's eye distraught,
Or hers before a looking-glass, for such,
Being made beautiful overmuch,
Consider beauty a sufficient end,
Lose natural kindness and maybe
The heart-revealing intimacy
That chooses right, and never find a friend.

Helen being chosen found life flat and dull
And later had much trouble from a fool,
While that great Queen, that rose out of the spray,
Being fatherless could have her way
Yet chose a bandy-leggèd smith for man.
It's certain that fine women eat
A crazy salad with their meat
Whereby the Horn of Plenty is undone.

In courtesy I'd have her chiefly learned;
Hearts are not had as a gift but hearts are earned
By those that are not entirely beautiful;
Yet many, that have played the fool
For beauty's very self, has charm made wise,
And many a poor man that has roved,
Loved and thought himself beloved,
From a glad kindness cannot take his eyes.

May she become a flourishing hidden tree
That all her thoughts may like the linnet be,
And have no business but dispensing round
Their magnanimities of sound,
Nor but in merriment begin a chase,
Nor but in merriment a quarrel.
O may she live like some green laurel
Rooted in one dear perpetual place.

My mind, because the minds that I have loved,
The sort of beauty that I have approved,
Prosper but little, has dried up of late,
Yet knows that to be choked with hate
May well be of all evil chances chief.
If there's no hatred in a mind
Assault and battery of the wind
Can never tear the linnet from the leaf.

An intellectual hatred is the worst,
So let her think opinions are accursed.
Have I not seen the loveliest woman born
Out of the mouth of Plenty's horn,
Because of her opinionated mind
Barter that horn and every good
By quiet natures understood
For an old bellows full of angry wind?

Considering that, all hatred driven hence,
The soul recovers radical innocence
And learns at last that it is self-delighting,
Self-appeasing, self-affrighting,
And that its own sweet will is Heaven's will;
She can, though every face should scowl
And every windy quarter howl
Or every bellows burst, be happy still.

And may her bridegroom bring her to a house
Where all's accustomed, ceremonious;
For arrogance and hatred are the wares
Peddled in the thoroughfares.
How but in custom and in ceremony
Are innocence and beauty born?
Ceremony's a name for the rich horn,
And custom for the spreading laurel tree.

A Song

I thought no more was needed
Youth to prolong
Than dumb-bell and foil
To keep the body young.
O who could have foretold
That the heart grows old?

Though I have many words,
What woman's satisfied,
I am no longer faint
Because at her side?
O who could have foretold
That the heart grows old?

I have not lost desire
But the heart that I had;
I thought 'twould burn my body
Laid on the death-bed,
For who could have foretold
That the heart grows old?

Leda and the Swan

A sudden blow: the great wings beating still
Above the staggering girl, her thighs caressed
By the dark webs, her nape caught in his bill,
He holds her helpless breast upon his breast.

How can those terrified vague fingers push
The feathered glory from her loosening thighs?
And how can body, laid in that white rush,
But feel the strange heart beating where it lies?

A shudder in the loins engenders there
The broken wall, the burning roof and tower
And Agamemnon dead.
                    Being so caught up,
So mastered by the brute blood of the air,
Did she put on his knowledge with his power
Before the indifferent beak could let her drop?

Byzantium

The unpurged images of day recede;
The Emperor's drunken soldiery are abed;
Night resonance recedes, night-walkers' song
After great cathedral gong;
A starlit or a moonlit dome disdains
All that man is,
All mere complexities,
The fury and the mire of human veins.

Before me floats an image, man or shade,
Shade more than man, more image than a shade
For Hades' bobbin bound in mummy-cloth
May unwind the winding path;
A mouth that has no moisture and no breath
Breathless mouths may summon;
I hail the superhuman;
I call it death-in-life and life-in-death.

Miracle, bird or golden handiwork,
More miracle than bird or handiwork,
Planted on the star-lit golden bough,
Can like the cocks of Hades crow,
Or, by the moon embittered, scorn aloud
In glory of changeless metal
Common bird or petal
And all complexities of mire or blood.

At midnight on the Emperor's pavement flit
Flames that no faggot feeds, nor steel has lit,
Nor storm disturbs, flames begotten of flame,
Where blood-begotten spirits come
And all complexities of fury leave,
Dying into a dance,
An agony of trance,
An agony of flame that cannot singe a sleeve.

Astraddle on the dolphin's mire and blood,
Spirit after spirit! The smithies break the flood,
The golden smithies of the Emperor!
Marbles of the dancing floor
Break bitter furies of complexity,
Those images that yet
Fresh images beget,
That dolphin-torn, that gong-tormented sea.

Long-Legged Fly

That civilisation may not sink,
Its great battle lost,
Quiet the dog, tether the pony
To a distant post;
Our master Cæsar is in the tent
Where the maps are spread,
His eyes fixed upon nothing,
A hand under his head.
Like a long-legged fly upon the stream
His mind moves upon silence.

That the topless towers be burnt
And men recall that face,
Move most gently if move you must
In this lonely place.
She thinks, part woman, three parts a child,
That nobody looks; her feet
Practise a tinker shuffle
Picked up on a street.
Like a long-legged fly upon the stream
Her mind moves upon silence.

That girls at puberty may find
The first Adam in their thought,
Shut the door of the Pope's chapel,

Keep those children out.
There on that scaffolding reclines
Michael Angelo.
With no more sound than the mice make
His hand moves to and fro.
Like a long-legged fly upon the stream
His mind moves upon silence.

The Circus Animals' Desertion

I

I sought a theme and sought for it in vain,
I sought it daily for six weeks or so.
Maybe at last, being but a broken man,
I must be satisfied with my heart, although
Winter and summer till old age began
My circus animals were all on show,
Those stilted boys, that burnished chariot,
Lion and woman and the Lord knows what.

II

What can I but enumerate old themes?
First that sea-rider Oisin led by the nose
Through three enchanted islands, allegorical dreams,
Vain gaiety, vain battle, vain repose,
Themes of the embittered heart, or so it seems,
That might adorn old songs or courtly shows;
But what cared I that set him on to ride,
I, starved for the bosom of his færy bride?

And then a counter-truth filled out its play,
The Countess Cathleen was the name I gave it;
She, pity-crazed, had given her soul away,
But masterful Heaven had intervened to save it.
I thought my dear must her own soul destroy,
So did fanaticism and hate enslave it,

And this brought forth a dream and soon enough
This dream itself had all my thought and love.

And when the Fool and Blind Man stole the bread
Cuchulain fought the ungovernable sea;
Heart-mysteries there, and yet when all is said
It was the dream itself enchanted me:
Character isolated by a deed
To engross the present and dominate memory.
Players and painted stage took all my love,
And not those things that they were emblems of.

III

Those masterful images because complete
Grew in pure mind, but out of what began?
A mound of refuse or the sweepings of a street,
Old kettles, old bottles, and a broken can,
Old iron, old bones, old rags, that raving slut
Who keeps the till. Now that my ladder's gone,
I must lie down where all the ladders start,
In the foul rag-and-bone shop of the heart.

LAURENCE BINYON

*Laurence Binyon was born in Lancaster in 1869 – he was a cousin
of Stephen Phillips – and educated at St Paul's School and Trinity
College, Oxford. He entered the service of the British Museum in
1893 and soon found himself in the Department of Prints and
Drawings. From 1913 to 1932 he was in charge of the sub-depart-
ment of Oriental Prints and Drawings, and he was Keeper of the
whole department 1932–3. In the following year he was Professor
of Poetry at Harvard University. He died in 1943.*

*Binyon was an authority on oriental art and a writer of books on
fine art, of plays, poems, and critical studies of literature. His*

Collected Poems *were issued in 1931, to be followed by* The North
Star and Other Poems *(1941) and the posthumous* The Burning
of the Leaves *(1944). The poem I have used is from this last
volume — a 'blitz' poem in the same restricted sense as parts of
Eliot's 'Little Gidding'.*

*Binyon seems to me a good example of an academic poet. He
does not, that is to say, extend the area of contemporary sensibility
or innovate technically, but he maintains with dignity the standards
he inherits. It is possible that he will be remembered longest for his
excellent translation of Dante's* Divina Commedia *into English
terza rima* (The Inferno *1933,* The Purgatorio *1938,* The
Paradiso *1943).*

The Burning of the Leaves

Now is the time for the burning of the leaves.
They go to the fire; the nostril pricks with smoke
Wandering slowly into the weeping mist.
Brittle and blotched, ragged and rotten sheaves!
A flame seizes the smouldering ruin, and bites
On stubborn stalks that crackle as they resist.

The last hollyhock's fallen tower is dust:
All the spices of June are a bitter reek,
All the extravagant riches spent and mean.
All burns! the reddest rose is a ghost.
Sparks whirl up, to expire in the mist: the wild
Fingers of fire are making corruption clean.

Now is the time for stripping the spirit bare,
Time for the burning of days ended and done,
Idle solace of things that have gone before,
Rootless hope and fruitless desire are there:
Let them go to the fire with never a look behind.
That world that was ours is a world that is ours no more

They will come again, the leaf and the flower, to arise
From squalor of rottenness into the old splendour,
And magical scents to a wondering memory bring;
The same glory, to shine upon different eyes.
Earth cares for her own ruins, naught for ours.
Nothing is certain, only the certain spring.

WALTER DE LA MARE

*Walter de la Mare was born in Kent in 1873 – he came of Hugue-
not stock – and was educated at St Paul's Cathedral Choir School.
He spent eighteen years in business before devoting himself entirely
to literature. His first book,* Songs of Childhood (*1902*), *was
published under a pseudonym, and his first prose book,* Henry
Brocken, *under his own name in 1904. He has a Civil List pension
for literary distinction and is a Fellow of the Royal Society of
Literature and an Hon. Litt.D. of Cambridge University. His*
Memoirs of a Midget (*1921*) *was awarded the James Tait Black
Prize. He is an anthologist of genius – see, for example,* Early One
Morning (*1935*), *which exploits his preoccupation with childhood,
and* Love (*1943*) *– and a short story writer whose powers of creating
an atmosphere, particularly the atmosphere of the uncanny, are
exceptional. Graham Greene has written illuminatingly on the short
stories in* A Tribute (*mentioned below*). *His best-known tales of the
supernatural are probably 'All Hallows' and 'Seaton's Aunt'.
Among his publications of poetry may be mentioned* Collected
Poems (*1942*), Collected Rhymes and Verses (*1944*), The
Burning Glass (*1945*), The Traveller (*1946*).*

*There is a study of his work by Forrest Reid published in 1922,
and in 1948 a volume entitled* A Tribute to Walter de la Mare *on
his 75th Birthday was brought out. This symposium is a useful*

introduction to his work as a whole. Mr Eliot's poem in it charac-
terizes the poetry of Walter de la Mare with precision:

> *By whom, and by what means, was this designed?*
> *The whispered incantation which allows*
> *Free passage to the phantoms of the mind.*
>
> *By you; by those deceptive cadences*
> *Wherewith the common measure is refined;*
> *By conscious art practised with natural ease.*

The poems given here are from Collected Poems *with the exception of 'A Portrait' from* The Burning Glass. *The long extract from 'Dreams' is at once a theory of composition and a kind of poetic apologia.*

The Children of Stare

> Winter is fallen early
>   On the house of Stare;
> Birds in reverberating flocks
>   Haunt its ancestral box;
>   Bright are the plenteous berries
>   In clusters in the air.
>
>   Still is the fountain's music,
>   The dark pool icy still,
> Whereupon a small and sanguine sun
>   Floats in a mirror on,
>   Into a West of crimson,
>   From a South of daffodil.
>
>   'Tis strange to see young children
>   In such a wintry house;
> Like rabbits' on the frozen snow
>   Their tell-tale footprints go;
>   Their laughter rings like timbrels
>   'Neath evening ominous:

Their small and heightened faces
Like wine-red winter buds;
Their frolic bodies gentle as
    Flakes in the air that pass,
    Frail as the twirling petal
    From the briar of the woods.

Above them silence lours,
    Still as an arctic sea;
Light fails; night falls; the wintry moon
    Glitters; the crocus soon
    Will open grey and distracted
    On earth's austerity:

Thick mystery, wild peril,
    Law like an iron rod:—
Yet sport they on in Spring's attire,
    Each with his tiny fire
    Blown to a core of ardour
    By the awful breath of God.

From *Dreams*

Was it by cunning the curious fly
That preys in a sunbeam schooled her wings
To ride her in air all motionlessly,
Poised on their myriad winnowing?
Where conned the blackbird the song he sings?
Was Job the instructor of the ant?
Go bees for nectar to Hume and Kant?

Who bade the scallop devise her shell?
Who tutored the daisy at cool of eve
To tent her pollen in floreted cell?
What dominie taught the dove to grieve;
The mole to delve; the worm to weave?
Does not the rather their life-craft seem
A tranced obedience to a dream?

Thus tranced, too, body and mind, will sit
A winter's dawn to dark, alone,
Heedless of how the cold moments flit,
The worker in words, or wood, or stone:
So far his waking desires have flown
Into a realm where his sole delight
Is to bring the dreamed-of to mortal sight.

Dumb in its wax may the music sleep –
In a breath conceived – that, with ardent care,
Note by note, in a reverie deep,
Mozart penned, for the world to share.
Waken it, needle! And then declare
How, invoked by thy tiny tang,
Sound such strains as the Sirens sang!

Voyager dauntless on Newton's sea,
Year after year still brooding on
His algebraical formulæ,
The genius of William Hamilton
Sought the square root of *minus* one;
In vain; till – all thought of it leagues away –
The problem flowered from a dream one day.

Our restless senses leap and say,
'How marvellous this! – How ugly that!'
And, at a breath, will slip away
The very thing they marvel at.
Time is the tyrant of their fate;
And frail the instant which must be
Our all of actuality.

If then to Solomon the Wise
Some curious priest stooped low and said,
'Thou, with thy lidded, sleep-sealed eyes,
This riddle solve from out thy bed:

Art thou – am I – by phantoms led?
Where is the real? In dream? Or wake?'
I know the answer the King might make!

And teeming Shakespeare: would he avow
The creatures of his heart and brain,
Whom, Prospero-like, he could endow
With all that mortal souls contain,
Mere copies that a fool can feign
Out of the tangible and seen? –
This the sole range of his demesne?

Ask not the Dreamer! See him run,
Listening a shrill and gentle neigh,
Foot into stirrup, he is up, he has won
Enchanted foothills far away.
Somewhere? Nowhere? Who need say?
So be it in secrecy of his mind
He some rare delectation find.

Ay, once I dreamed of an age-wide sea
Whereo'er three moons stood leper-bright;
And once – from agony set free –
I scanned within the womb of night,
A hollow inwoven orb of light,
Thrilling with beauty no tongue could tell,
And knew it for Life's citadel.

And – parable as strange – once, I
Was lured to a city whose every stone,
And harpy human hastening by
Were spawn and sport of fear alone –
By soulless horror enthralled, driven on:
Even the waters that, ebon-clear,
Coursed through its dark, raved only of *Fear!*

Enigmas these; but not the face,
Fashioned of sleep, which, still at gaze
Of daybreak eyes, I yet could trace,
Made lovelier in the sun's first rays;
Nor that wild voice which in amaze,
Wide-wok'n, I listened singing on –
All memory of the singer gone.

O Poesy, of wellspring clear,
Let no sad Science thee suborn,
Who art thyself its planisphere!
All knowledge is foredoomed, forlorn –
Of inmost truth and wisdom shorn –
Unless imagination brings
Its skies wherein to use its wings.

Two worlds have we: without; within;
But all that sense can mete and span,
Until it confirmation win
From heart and soul, is death to man.
Of grace divine his life began;
And – Eden empty proved – in deep
Communion with his spirit in sleep

The Lord Jehovah of a dream
Bade him, past all desire, conceive
What should his solitude redeem;
And, to his sunlit eyes, brought Eve.
Would that my day-wide mind could weave
Faint concept of the scene from whence
She awoke to Eden's innocence!

Starven with cares, like tares in wheat,
Wildered with knowledge, chilled with doubt,
The timeless self in vain must beat
Against its walls to hasten out

Whither the living waters fount;
And – evil and good no more at strife –
Seek love beneath the tree of life.

When then in memory I look back
To childhood's visioned hours I see
What now my anxious soul doth lack
Is energy in peace to be
At one with nature's mystery:
And Conscience less my mind indicts
For idle days than dreamless nights.

Sunk Lyonesse

In sea-cold Lyonesse,
When the Sabbath eve shafts down
On the roofs, walls, belfries
Of the foundered town,
The Nereids pluck their lyres
Where the green translucency beats,
And with motionless eyes at gaze
Make minstrelsy in the streets.
And the ocean water stirs
In salt-worn casemate and porch.
Plies the blunt-snouted fish
With fire in his skull for torch.
And the ringing wires resound;
And the unearthly lovely weep,
In lament of the music they make
In the sullen courts of sleep:
Whose marble flowers bloom for aye:
And – lapped by the moon-guiled tide –
Mock their carver with heart of stone,
Caged in his stone-ribbed side.

A Portrait

Old: yet unchanged; – still pottering in his thoughts;
Still eagerly enslaved by books and print;
Less plagued, perhaps, by rigid musts and oughts,
But no less frantic in vain argument;

Still happy as a child, with its small toys,
Over his inkpot and his bits and pieces, –
Life's arduous, fragile and ingenuous joys,
Whose charm failed never – nay, it even increases!

Ev'n happier in watch of bird or flower,
Rainbow in heaven, or bud on thorny spray,
A star-strewn nightfall, and that heart-break hour
Of sleep-drowsed senses between dawn and day;

Loving the light – laved eyes in those wild hues! –
And dryad twilight, and the thronging dark;
A Crusoe ravished by mere solitude –
And silence – edged with music's faintest *Hark!*

And any chance-seen face whose loveliness
Hovers, a mystery, between dream and real;
Things usual yet miraculous that bless
And overwell a heart that still can feel;

Haunted by questions no man answered yet;
Pining to leap from A clean on to Z;
Absorbed by problems which the wise forget;
Avid for fantasy – yet how staid a head!

Senses at daggers with his intellect;
Quick, stupid; vain, retiring; ardent, cold;
Faithful and fickle; rash and circumspect;
And never yet at rest in any fold;

Punctual at meals; a spendthrift, close as Scot;
Rebellious, tractable, childish – long gone grey!
Impatient, volatile, tongue wearying not –
Loose, too; which, yet, thank heaven, was taught to pray;

'Childish' indeed! – a waif on shingle shelf
Fronting the rippled sands, the sun, the sea;
And nought but his marooned precarious self
For questing consciousness and will-to-be;

A feeble venturer – in a world so wide!
So rich in action, daring, cunning, strife!
You'd think, poor soul, he had taken Sloth for bride, –
Unless the imagined is the breath of life;

Unless to speculate bring virgin gold,
And *Let's-pretend* can range the seven seas,
And dreams are not mere tales by idiot told,
And tongueless truth may hide in fantasies;

Unless the alone may their own company find,
And churchyards harbour phantoms 'mid their bones,
And even a daisy may suffice a mind
Whose bindweed can redeem a heap of stones;

Too frail a basket for so many eggs –
Loose-woven: Gosling? cygnet? Laugh or weep?
Or is the cup at richest in its dregs?
The actual realest on the verge of sleep?

One yet how often the prey of doubt and fear,
Of bleak despondence, stark anxiety;
Ardent for what is neither now nor here,
An Orpheus fainting for Eurydice;

Not yet inert, but with a tortured breast
At hint of that bleak gulf – his last farewell;
Pining for peace, assurance, pause and rest,
Yet slave to what he loves past words tó tell;

A foolish, fond old man, his bed-time nigh,
Who still at western window stays to win
A transient respite from the latening sky,
And scarce can bear it when the Sun goes in.

EDWARD THOMAS

*Edward Thomas was born in 1878 and educated at St Paul's School
and Lincoln College, Oxford. He was always a writer, but he first
wrote verse at the suggestion of the American poet, Robert Frost,
with whose work the poems of Thomas have many points of contact
in subject, mood and tone. He was then over thirty years old.
Wilfred Gibson's 'The Golden Room' refers to the company of
Georgian poets who met in July 1914 at 'the Old Nailshop':*

> *Our neighbours from The Gallows, Catherine
> And Lascelles Abercrombie; Rupert Brooke;
> Elinor and Robert Frost, living a while
> At Little Iddons, who'd brought over with them
> Helen and Edward Thomas ...*

*He had married much earlier in 1899, and the story of his courtship
and marriage is movingly told in Helen Thomas's* As It Was
(1926) and World Without End *(1931). He served in the Artists'
Rifles in World War I and was killed in action at Arras in 1917.*

> *Thomas lies
> 'Neath Vimy Ridge, where he, among his fellows
> Died, just as life had touched his lips to song.*

There is a memorial to him at Froxfield, Hampshire.

*Much of Thomas's published prose was bread-and-butter work –
topography and biography such as* The Heart of England *(1906),*
The South Country *(1909) and the studies of Borrow, Jefferies
and Maeterlinck; but even in his most occasional writing – he was
for a time a critic and essayist for the* Daily Chronicle *– there is
something to reward a reader with patience. His poetry is to be
found in* Collected Poems *(1920), which has a preface by Walter
de la Mare.*

*Edward Thomas can be classed as a Georgian only by accident.
He was, as Dr Leavis has remarked, ' a very original poet who
devoted great technical subtlety to the expression of a distinctively
modern sensibility'. Noteworthy in the poems is an acuteness of
sensation faithfully and modestly transcribed in unobtrusive, hesi-
tating rhythms and a diction which does not draw attention to itself.
'Old Man' has been well discussed in Chapter II of* New Bearings
in English Poetry *(1932) by F. R. Leavis. 'No One So Much As
You' is included as a love-poem; its gentleness, honesty and poig-
nancy belong peculiarly to Thomas.*

Old Man

Old Man, or Lad's-love – in the name there's nothing
To one that knows not Lad's-love, or Old Man,
The hoar-green feathery herb, almost a tree,
Growing with rosemary and lavender.
Even to one that knows it well, the names
Half decorate, half perplex, the thing it is :
At least, what that is clings not to the names
In spite of time. And yet I like the names.

The herb itself I like not, but for certain
I love it, as some day the child will love it
Who plucks a feather from the door-side bush
Whenever she goes in or out of the house.
Often she waits there, snipping the tips and shrivelling
The shreds at last on to the path, perhaps

Thinking, perhaps of nothing, till she sniffs
Her fingers and runs off. The bush is still
But half as tall as she, though it is as old;
So well she clips it. Not a word she says;
And I can only wonder how much hereafter
She will remember, with that bitter scent,
Of garden rows, and ancient damson trees
Topping a hedge, a bent path to a door,
A low thick bush beside the door, and me
Forbidding her to pick.

               As for myself,
Where first I met the bitter scent is lost.
I, too, often shrivel the grey shreds,
Sniff them and think and sniff again and try
Once more to think what it is I am remembering,
Always in vain. I cannot like the scent,
Yet I would rather give up others more sweet,
With no meaning, than this bitter one.

I have mislaid the key. I sniff the spray
And think of nothing; I see and I hear nothing;
Yet seem, too, to be listening, lying in wait
For what I should, yet never can, remember:
No garden appears, no path, no hoar-green bush
Of Lad's-love, or Old Man, no child beside,
Neither father nor mother, nor any playmate;
Only an avenue, dark, nameless, without end.

No One So Much As You

No one so much as you
Loves this my clay,
Or would lament as you
Its dying day.

You know me through and through
Though I have not told,
And though with what you know
You are not bold.

None ever was so fair
As I thought you:
Not a word can I bear
Spoken against you.

All that I ever did
For you seemed coarse
Compared with what I hid
Nor put in force.

My eyes scarce dare meet you
Lest they should prove
I but respond to you
And do not love.

We look and understand,
We cannot speak
Except in trifles and
Words the most weak.

For I at most accept
Your love, regretting
That is all: I have kept
Only a fretting

That I could not return
All that you gave
And could not ever burn
With the love you have,

Till sometimes it did seem
Better it were

Never to see you more
Than linger here

With only gratitude
Instead of love –
A pine in solitude
Cradling a dove.

HAROLD MONRO

Harold Monro was born at Brussels in 1879 and lived there till the age of seven when his family moved to Wells in Somerset. He was educated at Radley and Caius College, Cambridge, and later spent some years in Ireland, Italy and Switzerland. In Florence he met the novelist Maurice Hewlett, who encouraged him in his ideas of writing and promoting poetry. He founded the famous Poetry Bookshop (which was responsible for the collections of Georgian Poetry *edited by Edward Marsh) in 1913 and produced* The Chapbook *(1919–25), which succeeded earlier periodicals such as* The Poetry Review *and* Poetry *and* Drama. *His anthology* Twentieth Century Poetry *(1929), a not too successful attempt at being catholic in taste, nevertheless introduced many ordinary readers to the more interesting modern poets and rightly excluded the usual 'show-poems', as Monro calls them. He died in 1932 and the* Collected Poems *were edited by his wife, Alida Monro, in 1933. The book contains a biographical sketch by the Imagist poet F. S. Flint and a critical note by T. S. Eliot.*

Some of Harold Monro's work has the weaknesses of Georgian poetry, but at his best he is saved from the mawkishness, clumsiness and/or namby-pambiness of the Masefields, Drinkwaters, Hodgsons, etc. by his thoughtfulness and 'awkward sincerity'. 'Living,' one of his strongest poems in my view, was a favourite with the poet according to Mrs Monro.

Living

Slow bleak awakening from the morning dream
Brings me in contact with the sudden day.
I am alive – this I.
I let my fingers move along my body.
Realisation warns them, and my nerves
Prepare their rapid messages and signals.
While Memory begins recording, coding,
Repeating; all the time Imagination
Mutters; You'll only die.

Here's a new day. O Pendulum move slowly!
My usual clothes are waiting on their peg.
I am alive – this I.
And in a moment Habit, like a crane,
Will bow its neck and dip its pulleyed cable,
Gathering me, my body, and our garment,
And swing me forth, oblivious of my question,
Into the daylight – why?

I think of all the others who awaken,
And wonder if they go to meet the morning
More valiantly than I;
Nor asking of this Day they will be living:
What have I done that I should be alive?
O, can I not forget that I am living?
How shall I reconcile the two conditions:
Living, and yet – to die?

Between the curtains the autumnal sunlight
With lean and yellow fingers points me out;
The clock moans: Why? Why? Why?
But suddenly, as if without a reason,
Heart, Brain and Body, and Imagination
All gather in tumultuous joy together,
Running like children down the path of morning

To fields where they can play without a quarrel:
A country I'd forgotten, but remember,
And welcome with a cry.

O cool glad pasture; living tree, tall corn,
Great cliff, or languid sloping sand, cold sea,
Waves; rivers curving: you, eternal flowers,
Give me content, while I can think of you:
Give me your living breath!
Back to your rampart, Death.

JAMES JOYCE

*James Joyce was born in Dublin in 1882 and was educated at
Clongowes Wood College, Belvedere College and University
College, Dublin. He was teaching languages at a Berlitz Institute
in Trieste in 1904, and thenceforth lived in self-imposed exile from
Ireland on the continent, a sort of cultural 'wild goose'. In Paris,
where he published his more important works, he was for many
years a tutelary deity of the magazine* Transition. *After the out-
break of war in 1939 he went to live in Switzerland where he died in
January, 1941. For fuller details of his life reference may be made
to* James Joyce: a definitive biography (*1941*) *by Herbert S.
Gorman, but the important part of his life is his books:* Dubliners
(*1914*), Portrait of the Artist as a Young Man (*1916*), Ulysses
(*1925*), *and* Finnegan's Wake (*1939*). *There is a study of the first
of the two major works by Stuart Gilbert –* James Joyce's Ulysses
(*1930*) *– and a useful analysis of the second,* A Skeleton Key to
Finnegan's Wake (*1947*) *by J. Campbell and H. M. Robinson.
The best book for the Joyce beginner is* Introducing James Joyce
(*1942*), *selections edited by T. S. Eliot. There is some acute
criticism of Joyce in Eliot's* After Strange Gods (*1934*).

From the books of verse produced by Joyce, Chamber Music *and*
Pomes Penyeach, *it is impossible to take the novelist very seriously
as a poet, but 'The Ballad of Persse O'Reilly' is in a different class*

It is written in the language of Finnegan's Wake, *which is a kind of 'Babylonish dialect' – a phrase used by Dr Johnson in speaking of Milton's language in* Paradise Lost. *Mr Eliot has pointed out the parallel between the blind and musically gifted Milton and the blind and musically gifted Joyce. Joyce's blindness or near-blindness forced him away from the visual to the musical and emotional associations of words, and his linguistic erudition supplied another element for the construction of the language of* Finnegan's Wake. *I think it probable that this book, over which Joyce spent sixteen years, will exercise an increasing influence as it is more intelligently studied and better understood. Auden's* Age of Anxiety *shows the power of Joyce's emotional rhetoric by direct imitation at several points—see 'The Seven Stages' passim and Rosetta's final soliloquy.*

Finnegan's Wake – *'a compound of fable, symphony and nightmare' (Campbell and Robinson) – is an allegory on many planes of 'the fall and resurrection of mankind'. The 'hero' is* H. C. Earwicker, *a Dublin tavern-keeper in Chapelizod whose universal quality is indicated by the names* Here Comes Everybody *and* Haveth Childers Everywhere. *He is a candidate in a local election, but he loses his reputation as a result of some never quite defined impropriety in Phoenix Park and suffers from the guilt of it ever afterwards. In another context of meaning Phoenix Park is the Garden of Eden and the impropriety is Original Sin. Three down-and-outs, Peter Cloran, O'Mara and Hosty, 'an illstarred beachbusker', pick up the rumour of Earwicker's Fall and Hosty lampoons him in the 'rann', 'The Ballad of Persse O'Reilly'. Note that* perce-oreille = *earwig.*

The Ballad of Persse O'Reilly

Have you heard of one Humpty Dumpty
How he fell with a roll and a rumble
And curled up like Lord Olofa Crumple
By the butt of the Magazine Wall,
    (*Chorus*) Of the Magazine Wall,
             Hump, helmet and all?

He was one time our King of the Castle
Now he's kicked about like a rotten old parsnip.
And from Green street he'll be sent by order of His Worship
To the penal jail of Mountjoy
> (*Chorus*) To the jail of Mountjoy!
>> Jail him and joy.

He was fafafather of all schemes for to bother us
Slow coaches and immaculate contraceptives for the populace,
Mare's milk for the sick, seven dry Sundays a week,
Openair love and religion's reform,
> (*Chorus*) And religious reform,
>> Hideous in form.

Arrah, why, says you, couldn't he manage it?
I'll go bail, my fine dairyman darling,
Like the bumping bull of the Cassidys
All your butter is in your horns.
> (*Chorus*) His butter is in his horns.
>> Butter his horns!

(*Repeat*) Hurrah there, Hosty, frosty Hosty, change that shirt
on ye,
Rhyme the rann, the king of all ranns!

> *Balbaccio, balbuccio!*

We had chaw chaw chops, chairs, chewing gum, the chicken-
pox and china chambers
Universally provided by this soffsoaping salesman.
Small wonder He'll Cheat E'erawan our local lads nicknamed
him
When Chimpden first took the floor
> (*Chorus*) With his bucketshop store
>> Down Bargainweg, Lower.

So snug he was in his hotel premises sumptuous
But soon we'll bonfire all his trash, tricks and trumpery
And 'tis short till sheriff Clancy'll be winding up his unlimited
      company
With the bailiff's bom at the door,
      (*Chorus*) Bimbam at the door.
                  Then he'll bum no more.

Sweet bad luck on the waves washed to our island
The hooker of that hammerfast viking
And Gall's curse on the day when Eblana bay
Saw his black and tan man-o'-war.
      (*Chorus*) Saw his man-o'-war
                  On the harbour bar.

Where from? roars Poolbeg. Cookingha'pence, he bawls
      Donnez-moi scampitle, wick an wipin'fampiny
Fingal Mac Oscar Onesine Bargearse Boniface
Thok's min gammelhole Norveegickers moniker
Og as ay are at gammelhore Norveegickers cod.
      (*Chorus*) A Norwegian camel old cod.
                  He is, begod.

Lift it, Hosty, lift it, ye devil ye! up with the rann, the rhyming
      rann!

It was during some fresh water garden pumping
Or, according to the *Nursing Mirror*, while admiring the
      monkeys
That our heavyweight heathen Humpharey
Made bold a maid to woo
      (*Chorus*) Woohoo, what'll she doo!
                  The general lost her maidenloo!

He ought to blush for himself, the old hayheaded philosopher,
For to go and shove himself that way on top of her.
Begob, he's the crux of the catalogue
Of our antediluvial zoo,
  (*Chorus*) Messrs. Billing and Coo.
    Noah's larks, good as noo.

He was joulting by Wellinton's monument
Our rotorious hippopopotamuns
When some bugger let down the backtrap of the omnibus
And he caught his death of fusiliers
  (*Chorus*) With his rent in his rears.
    Give him six years.

'Tis sore pity for his innocent poor children
But look out for his missus legitimate!
When that frew gets a grip of old Earwicker
Won't there be earwigs on the green?
  (*Chorus*) Big earwigs on the green,
    The largest ever you seen.

  Suffoclose! Shikespower! Seudodanto! Anonymoses!

Then we'll have a free trade Gaels' band and mass meeting
For to sod the brave son of Scandiknavery.
And we'll bury him down in Oxmanstown
Along with the devil and Danes,
  (*Chorus*) With the deaf and dumb Danes,
    And all their remains.

And not all the king's men nor his horses
Will resurrect his corpus
For there's no true spell in Connacht or hell
  (*bis*) That's able to raise a Cain.

WYNDHAM LEWIS

Wyndham Lewis was born in the U.S.A. in 1884 and educated in England at Rugby and the Slade School. He is a painter, novelist, sociologist, literary critic and several other things as well as a poet. What he wants the public to know about himself can be discovered by reading his entertaining autobiography, Blasting and Bombardiering *(1937), a book full of asides about the 'twenties and 'thirties and their main literary figures — Mr Eliot appears as 'a sleek, tall, attractive transatlantic apparition with a sort of Gioconda smile'. Among Lewis's novels may be mentioned* Tarr *(1918) and the incomplete* Childermass *(1928); among his books of general criticism,* Time and the Western Man *(1927); and among books of literary criticism,* The Lion and the Fox *(on Shakespeare) and* Men Without Art *(1934).* One-Way Song, *his only book of verse, appeared in 1933 and was intelligently praised by Gilbert Armitage in* New Verse *(No. 7, February 1934), but it was hardly understood at all by most reviewers. The Lewisian standpoint baffled them, quite apart from the 'normal' difficulty the average reviewer has with satire as poetry.*

Wyndham Lewis has kindly furnished me with the following notes on the writing of One-Way Song *(1) and on verse-satire (2). I print them as I received them.*

(1) 'Many people have enquired how it was that I, novelist, pamphleteer, sociologist and so on, suddenly took it into my head to produce a volume of verse. The answer is very simple: I was in the first place, and for years, when young, a writer of verse. One fine day I took it into my head to write a novel. So the enquiry, if at all, should be framed the other way round. Also, however, I was a painter — one strangely "advanced" for 1913; also I lived in Great Britain. It follows that I found it necessary to become a pamphleteer to defend my paintings against attack and a critic that I might expound the doctrines responsible for the difficulties that so bewildered and angered the public. Then I was a soldier and understood

war undoubtedly better than men who had not been that and years afterwards wrote pamphlet-books against new wars (but there are always new wars!). Many other things: books upon "Time" and upon how men can best manage their rulers. But one fine day I did think I would again express myself in verse. Hence One-Way Song.'

(2) '*Verse-satire, in which class* One-Way Song, *I imagine, would be found, belongs to the comic muse. It is far more at home in France than in this country, where Satire must always remain a scandal, and verse be regarded as an occasion for something "rather lovely", rather than something hideously true, or blisteringly witty. Certainly Mr Eliot in the 'twenties was responsible for a great vogue for verse-satire. An ideal formula of ironic, gently "satiric", self-expression was provided by that master for the undergraduate underworld, tired and thirsty for poetic fame in a small way. The results of Mr Eliot are not Mr Eliot himself: but satire with him has been the painted smile of the clown. Habits of expression ensuing from that mannerism are, as a fact, remote from the central function of satire.*

'*In its essence the purpose of satire — whether verse or prose — is aggression. (When whimsical, sentimental, or "poetic", it is a sort of bastard humour.) Satire has a great big glaring target. If successful, it blasts a great big hole in the centre. Directness there must be and singleness of aim: it is all aim, all trajectory. In that sense* One-Way Song *would only be found to answer the description "satiric verse" in certain sections. In those sections it is, I believe, at least authentic satire.*'

If So the Man You Are, 14

The man I am to blow the bloody gaff
If I were given platforms? The riff-raff
May be handed all the trumpets that you will.
Not so the golden-tongued. The window-sill
Is all the pulpit they can hope to get,

Of a slum-garret, sung by Mistinguette,
Too high up to be heard, too poor to attract
Anyone to their so-called 'scurrilous' tract.
What wind an honest mind advances? Look
No wind of sickle and hammer, of bell and book,
No wind of any party, or blowing out
Of any mountain hemming us about
Of 'High Finance', or the foothills of same.
The man I am who does *not* play the game!
Of these incalculable ones I am
Not to be trusted with free-speech to damn,
To be given enough rope – just enough to hang.
To be hobbled in a dry field. As the bird sang
Who punctured poor Cock Robin, by some sparrow
Condemned to be shot at with toy bow and arrow.
You will now see how it stands with all of those
Who strong propensities for truth disclose.
It's no use buddy – you are for it boy
If not from head to foot a pure alloy!
If so the man you are that lets the cat
Out of the bag, you're a marked fellow and that's flat.

One-Way Song, XXIV

In any medium except that of verse
Forthwith I could enlighten you. Too terse,
And as it were compact, this form of art –
Which handles the finished product only – the hard
Master-material of selected sound.
The intellect has its workshops underground;
We cannot go back, out of this dance of words,
To become the teacher. Here we behave as birds –
The brain-that-sweats *offends*, it breaks our spell,
You do see that? we really must not *smell*
In this role: it is aristocratic but

Cudgel your brains in this case you must *not*.
So you will understand that argument,
Except in intent stylistic, or to invent
A certain pattern, is out of the question here.
I can only release, as elegant as deer,
A herd of wandering shapes, which *may* go straight,
But are just as likely to have grandly strayed,
Before we write finis out of sight and reach.
I cannot help this. It is noblesse oblige.

D. H. LAWRENCE

David Herbert Lawrence, the son of a coal-miner, was born at Eastwood in Nottinghamshire in 1885 and educated at Notttingham High School and University College, Nottingham. There is a large, probably too large, Lawrence literature, so that it is only necessary to note a few salient facts of his life: his qualifying as a school teacher — one of his best 'rhyming' poems is 'The Last Lesson of the Afternoon'; his marriage in 1914; his travels in Italy, New Mexico and Australia (v. Twilight in Italy [1916], Sea and Sardinia [1921], Mornings in Mexico [1927]); and his death of consumption near Nice in 1930. His reputation as a novelist was made with The White Peacock *(1911) and* Sons and Lovers *(1913).* The Rainbow *(1915) was the subject of a police prosecution. Later novels of importance are* Women in Love *(1921),* Aaron's Rod *(1922),* Kangaroo *(1923) and* Lady Chatterley's Lover *(1928), of which a bowdlerized edition appeared in England in 1932. His* Collected Poems *were published in 1928, to be followed in 1933 by* Last Poems, *edited by Richard Aldington. Lawrence's* Letters, *edited by Aldous Huxley with a useful introduction, were issued in 1932.*

'The Mosquito' is one of the less familiar pieces of 'Birds, Beasts and Flowers', a section of his Collected Poems *containing a high proportion of his best work. These pieces, Lawrence tells us, 'were begun in Tuscany, in the autumn of 1920, and finished in New*

Mexico in 1923, in my thirty-eighth year'. 'Bavarian Gentians' is from Last Poems. *Both of these poems are in free verse — I use that term not in the sense of a divagation from the norm of the blank verse line more extreme than that practised by the Jacobean dramatists (v. Eliot's Introduction to Ezra Pound's* Selected Poems, *1928), but in the other recognized sense of a cadenced form of writing, buttressed with repetitions, parallelisms and occasional rhymes, derived directly from Whitman and beyond him from the translators of the metrical portions of the Bible. This has been defended as a highway of poetic development by Herbert Read, but it seems to me to be a cul-de-sac: except in the hands of a Lawrence the writing is liable to be diffuse and to sprawl, and even in his hands the poems seem only gradually to warm into life. Too much attention has to be given to rhythm when form is so fluid; and this seems to correlate with a lack of verbal sparkle and excitement. The third poem, 'Innocent England', celebrates Lawrence's contempt and indignation at the suppression of his exhibition of paintings in London in 1928: the authorities feared for public morals because he painted pubic hair on his nudes.*

Louis MacNeice in a journalistic, provocative 'Alphabet of Literary Prejudices' remarks under the heading 'Dark God':

> *As D. H. Lawrence was well slapped down in the 'twenties by Mr Wyndham Lewis there is no need now to take another slap at one who, in spite of his unfortunate effect on adolescents, was a great writer and a godsend ... Lawrence had imagination without commonsense — and got away with it — but in most people this divorce will degrade imagination itself.*

I should add that I consider 'The Mosquito' an excellent poem. The other two pieces achieve what they set out to do and are, in their different ways, good.

The Mosquito

When did you start your tricks,
Monsieur?

What do you stand on such high legs for?
Why this length of shredded shank,
You exaltation?

Is it so that you shall lift your centre of gravity upwards
And weigh no more than air as you alight upon me,
Stand upon me weightless, you phantom?

I heard a woman call you the Winged Victory
In sluggish Venice.
You turn your head towards your tail, and smile.

How can you put so much devilry
Into that translucent phantom shred
Of a frail corpus?

Queer, with your thin wings and your streaming legs,
How you sail like a heron, or a dull clot of air,
A nothingness.

Yet what an aura surrounds you;
Your evil little aura, prowling, and casting a numbness on my
    mind.

That is your trick, your bit of filthy magic:
Invisibility, and the anæsthetic power
To deaden my attention in your direction.

But I know your game now, streaky sorcerer.

Queer, how you stalk and prowl the air
In circles and evasions, enveloping me,
Ghoul on wings
Winged Victory.

Settle, and stand on long thin shanks
Eyeing me sideways, and cunningly conscious that I am aware,
You speck.

I hate the way you lurch off sideways into air
Having read my thoughts against you.

Come then, let us play at unawares,
And see who wins in this sly game of bluff.
Man or mosquito.

You don't know that I exist, and I don't know that you exist.
Now then!

It is your trump,
It is your hateful little trump,
You pointed fiend,
Which shakes my sudden blood to hatred of you:
It is your small, high, hateful bugle in my ear.

Why do you do it?
Surely it is bad policy.

They say you can't help it.

If that is so, then I believe a little in Providence protecting the
    innocent.
But it sounds so amazingly like a slogan,
A yell of triumph as you snatch my scalp.

Blood, red blood
Super-magical
Forbidden liquor.

I behold you stand
For a second enspasmed in oblivion,
Obscenely ecstasied
Sucking live blood,
My blood.

Such silence, such suspended transport,
Such gorging,
Such obscenity of trespass.

You stagger
As well as you may.
Only your accursed hairy frailty,
Your own imponderable weightlessness
Saves you, wafts you away on the very draught my anger makes
    in its snatching.

Away with a pæan of derision,
You winged blood-drop.

Can I not overtake you?
Are you one too many for me,
Winged Victory?
Am I not mosquito enough to out-mosquito you?

Queer, what a big stain my sucked blood makes
Beside the infinitesimal faint smear of you!
Queer, what a dim dark smudge you have disappeared into!

Bavarian Gentians

Not every man has gentians in his house
in Soft September, at slow, Sad Michaelmas.

Bavarian gentians, big and dark, only dark
darkening the day-time torch-like with the smoking blueness of
    Pluto's gloom,
ribbed and torch-like, with their blaze of darkness spread blue
down flattening into points, flattened under the sweep of white
    day

torch-flower of the blue-smoking darkness, Pluto's dark-blue
    daze,
black lamps from the halls of Dis, burning dark blue,
giving off darkness, blue darkness, as Demeter's pale lamps give
    off light,
lead me then, lead me the way.

Reach me a gentian, give me a torch
let me guide myself with the blue, forked torch of this flower
down the darker and darker stairs, where blue is darkened on
    blueness,
even where Persephone goes, just now, from the frosted
    September
to the sightless realm where darkness is awake upon the dark
and Persephone herself is but a voice
or a darkness invisible enfolded in the deeper dark
of the arms Plutonic, and pierced with the passion of dense
    gloom,
among the splendour of torches of darkness, shedding darkness
    on the lost bride and her groom.

Innocent England

Oh what a pity, Oh! don't you agree
that figs aren't found in the land of the free!

Fig-trees don't grow in my native land;
there's never a fig-leaf near at hand

when you want one; so I did without;
and that is what the row's about.

Virginal, pure policemen came
and hid their faces for very shame,

while they carried the shameless things away
to gaol, to be hid from the light of day.

And Mr. Mead, that old, old lily
said: 'Gross! coarse! hideous!' – and I, like a silly

thought he meant the faces of the police-court officials,
and how right he was, and I signed my initials

to confirm what he said: but alas, he meant
my pictures, and on the proceedings went.

The upshot was, my pictures must burn
that English artists might finally learn

when they painted a nude, to put a *cache sexe* on,
a cache sexe, a cache sexe, or else begone!

A fig-leaf; or, if you cannot find it
a wreath of mist, with nothing behind it.

A wreath of mist is the usual thing
in the north, to hide where the turtles sing.

Though they never sing, they never sing,
don't you dare to suggest such a thing

or Mr Mead will be after you.
– But what a pity I never knew

A wreath of English mist would do
as a cache sexe! I'd have put a whole fog.

But once and forever barks the old dog,
so my pictures are in prison, instead of in the Zoo.

ANDREW YOUNG

Andrew Young was born in Elgin in 1885 and educated at Edinburgh University where he took the degree of M.A. He came south in 1920 to live in Hove and is now Vicar of Stonegate, Sussex, and Canon of Chichester Cathedral. He is well known as an authority on wild flowers. He published a volume of Collected Poems *in 1936, and later volumes are* Speak to the Earth *(1939), from which I reprint 'A Prospect of Death', and* The Green Man *(1947). He is also the author of a prose work,* A Prospect of Flowers, *and of a play in verse,* Nicodemus *(1937). Of his work Edwin Muir has said justly that it is metaphysical in turn, has a mastery of detail and is 'never trivial and never commonplace'.*

A Prospect of Death

If it should come to this,
You cannot wake me with a kiss,
Think I but sleep too late
Or once again keep a cold angry state.

So now you have been told;
I or my breakfast may grow cold,
But you must only say
'Why does he miss the best part of the day?'

Even then you may be wrong;
Through woods torn by a blackbird's song
My thoughts will often roam
While graver business makes me stay at home.

There will be time enough
To go back to the earth I love
Some other day that week,
Perhaps to find what all my life I seek.

So do not dream of danger;
Forgive my lateness or my anger;
You have so much forgiven,
Forgive me this or that, or Hell or Heaven.

CHARLES WILLIAMS

Charles Williams was born in London in 1886 and educated at St Albans Grammar School and University College, London. He was a member of the staff of the London branch of the Oxford University Press for thirty-six years, and it was while he worked there that he wrote his novels, criticism and poetry. He lectured at the City of London Literary Institute, and during the Second World War made a reputation at Oxford as a lecturer and private tutor. He died in May 1945.

His novels may be described fairly as supernatural thrillers and include two which have been widely read: War in Heaven *and* All Hallows Eve. *Better known still, at least by literary students, are* The English Poetic Mind (*1932*) *and* The Figure of Beatrice (*1943*). *Another influential prose book by Charles Williams is* The Descent of the Dove (*1939*), *which has the sub-title 'A Short History of the Holy Spirit in the Church'. Some of his poetry was published as early as 1917, but his present reputation and influence rest on* Taliessin Through Logres (*1938*) *and* The Region of the Summer Stars (*1944*).

Arthurian Torso (1948), *containing the prose fragment 'The Figure of Arthur' by Charles Williams and an ingenious commentary by C. S. Lewis on Williams's Arthurian poems, is necessary reading for anyone hoping to grasp the ideas behind and the meaning of the two mature poetic works listed above. 'The Calling of Arthur' is reprinted from* Taliessin Through Logres. *In this poem Merlin calls Arthur to his inheritance, the throne which has to be seized from Cradlemas, King of London, 'the last feeble, fragile and sinister representative of Roman civilization' with his emerald monocle, gilded mask and pretended pity for his miserable subjects. It is an early and comparatively straightforward poem in the Arthurian sequence – this is my reason for selecting it – and in the view of Mr C. S. Lewis one of the best as word-music. 'There are poems in which Williams has produced word music equalled by only two or three in this century and surpassed by none. "The Calling of Arthur" responds metrically to every movement of the emotion ...' While I agree that this poem is in rhythm and melody one of the best in the two Arthurian volumes, the first part of this statement seems to me to be quite groundless. I also consider Mr Lewis's general estimate of the importance of Charles Williams as a poet wildly off the mark.*

It would be unfair to leave such a remark without some explanation. Like other writers, Mr Lewis has in my opinion been hypnotized by his memories of the man, and by his conviction of the importance and wisdom of the things Williams had to say, into imagining that they are said (and happily) in the poems. The truth is that these things are barely half-said: all Mr Lewis's ingenuity is needed to disentangle even the story, and the full 'philosophical' meaning is still further to seek. Again, it seems to me that the honesty of the writer does not prevent him at times from being metrically clumsy and in expression uncouth and, more rarely, bathetic. In sum, I think the poems are a literary oddity of great interest, and I include one of them because the influence of Williams's personality and ideas – including poetic ideas – on Eliot, Auden and younger writers such as Anne Ridler is admitted. I think the effect of his poetry – simply as poetry – has been and will be negligible.

The Calling of Arthur

Arthur was young; Merlin met him on the road.
    Wolfish, the wizard stared, coming from the wild,
    black with hair, bleak with hunger, defiled
from a bed in the dung of cattle, inhuman his eyes.

Bold stood Arthur; the snow beat; Merlin spoke:
    Now am I Camelot; now am I to be builded.
    King Cradlemas sits by Thames; a mask o'ergilded
covers his wrinkled face, all but one eye.

Cold and small he settles his rump in the cushions.
    Through the emerald of Nero one short-sighted eye
    peers at the pedlars of wealth that stand plausibly by.
The bleak mask is gilded with a maiden's motionless smile.

The high aged voice squeals with callous comfort.
    He sits on the bank of Thames, a sea-snail's shell
    fragile, fragilely carved, cast out by the swell
on to the mud; his spirit withers and dies.

He withers; he peers at the tide; he squeals.
    He warms himself by the fire and eats his food
    through a maiden's motionless mouth; in his mood
he polishes his emerald, misty with tears for the poor.

The waste of snow covers the waste of thorn;
    on the waste of hovels snow falls from a dreary sky;
    mallet and scythe are silent; the children die.
King Cradlemas fears that the winter is hard for the poor.

Draw now the tide, spring morn, swing now the depth;
    under the snow that falls over brick and prickle,
    the people ebb; draw up the hammer and sickle.
The banner of Bors is abroad; where is the king?

Bors is up; his wife Elayne behind him
    mends the farms, gets food from Gaul; the south
    is up with hammer and sickle, and holds Thames mouth.
Lancelot hastens, coming with wagons and ships.

The sea-snail lies by Thames; O wave of Pendragon,
    roll it, swallow it; pull the mask o'ergilded
    from the one-eyed face that blinks at the comfort builded
in London's ruins; I am Camelot; Arthur, raise me.

Arthur ran; the people marched; in the snow
    King Cradlemas died in his litter; a screaming few
    fled; Merlin came; Camelot grew.
In Logres the King's friend landed, Lancelot of Gaul.

SIEGFRIED SASSOON

*Siegfried Sassoon was born in 1886 and educated at Marlborough
and Clare College, Cambridge. He served with the Sussex Yeo-
manry and the Royal Welch Fusiliers in France and Palestine
during World War I and won the M.C. He was in hospital at
Craiglockhart with Wilfred Owen, who wrote of him enthusiasti-
cally 'as a man; as a friend and a poet':*

> *Know that since mid-September, when you still regarded
> me as a tiresome little knocker on your door, I hold you as
> Keats + Christ + Elijah + my Colonel + my father-con-
> fessor + Amenophis IV in profile.*

The hospital magazine, The Hydra, *printed verse by both poets.
Another picture of Sassoon during the war can be found in* Goodbye
to All That *by Robert Graves.*

In 1919 Sassoon was literary editor of the Daily Herald. *His prose work,* The Complete Memoirs of George Sherston, *was published in 1937 – he had received the Hawthornden Prize and the James Tait Black Memorial Prize for the first part of it –* The Memoirs of a Fox-hunting Man, *in 1929.* The Complete Memoirs *compose a semi-autobiographical narrative, which can be supplemented by* Siegfried's Journey *(1945). The* Collected Poems *appeared in 1946, and Sassoon's most recent publication is a biography of Meredith (1948).*

I have represented the poet here by pieces written during the First and Second World Wars ('The Death-Bed' and 'The Child at the Window'). Originally I chose 'Repression of War Experience' to stand for his early work, but Mr Sassoon considers it a period-piece already as a 'war-protest' poem and suggested 'The Death-Bed' in its place as 'a better bit of verse'. He remarks of his own poetry that it 'belongs to the pre-Eliot period in technique and expression'.

The Death-Bed

He drowsed and was aware of silence heaped
Round him, unshaken as the steadfast walls;
Aqueous like floating rays of amber light,
Soaring and quivering in the wings of sleep.
Silence and safety; and his mortal shore
Lipped by the inward, moonless waves of death.

Someone was holding water to his mouth.
He swallowed, unresisting; moaned and dropped
Through crimson gloom to darkness; and forgot
The opiate throb and ache that was his wound.
    Water – calm, sliding green above the weir.
    Water – a sky-lit alley for his boat,
    Bird-voiced, and bordered with reflected flowers
    And shaken hues of summer; drifting down,
    He dipped contented oars, and sighed, and slept.

Night, with a gust of wind, was in the ward,
Blowing the curtain to a glimmering curve.
Night. He was blind; he could not see the stars
Glinting among the wraiths of wandering cloud;
Queer blots of colour, purple, scarlet, green,
Flickered and faded in his drowning eyes.

Rain – he could hear it rustling through the dark;
Fragrance and passionless music woven as one;
Warm rain on drooping roses; pattering showers
That soak the woods; not the harsh rain that sweeps
Behind the thunder, but a trickling peace,
Gently and slowly washing life away.

．　　　．　　　．　　　．

He stirred, shifting his body; then the pain
Leapt like a prowling beast, and gripped and tore
His groping dreams with grinding claws and fangs.
But someone was beside him; soon he lay
Shuddering because that evil thing had passed.
And death, who'd stepped toward him, paused and stared

Light many lamps and gather round his bed.
Lend him your eyes, warm blood, and will to live.
Speak to him; rouse him; you may save him yet.
He's young; he hated War; how should he die
When cruel old campaigners win safe through?

But death replied: 'I choose him'. So he went,
And there was silence in the summer night;
Silence and safety; and the veils of sleep.
Then, far away, the thudding of the guns.

The Child at the Window

Remember this, when childhood's far away;
The sunlight of a showery first spring day;
You from your house-top window laughing down,
And I, returned with whip-cracks from a ride,
On the great lawn below you, playing the clown.
Time blots our gladness out. Let this with love abide...

The brave March day; and you, not four years old,
Up in your nursery world – all heaven for me.
Remember this – the happiness I hold –
In far off springs I shall not live to see;
The world one map of wastening war unrolled,
And you, unconscious of it, setting my spirit free.

For you must learn, beyond bewildering years,
How little things beloved and held are best.
The windows of the world are blurred with tears,
And troubles come like cloud-banks from the west.
Remember this, some afternoon in spring,
When your own child looks down and makes your sad heart
    sing.

EDWIN MUIR

Edwin Muir was born at Deerness in the Orkneys in 1887 and educated at Kirkwall Burgh School until the age of fourteen. After this he became a clerk in commercial and shipbuilding firms in Glasgow. In 1919 he married Willa Anderson and settled in London as a free-lance journalist; from 1919 to 1921 he was assistant-editor of The New Age; *and in 1921 he went with his wife to Prague. From then until 1928 he lived 'nomadically' on the continent, becoming known at the same time in this country as a poet, critic and translator. His translations (with Willa Muir) of*

Kafka introduced that writer to English audiences. After 1934 he became co-editor of the European Quarterly, *and he was until recently Director of the British Institute in Prague. An autobiography,* The Story and the Fable, *was published in 1940.*

Among his collections of poems may be noted: First Poems (*1925*), Variations on a Time Theme (*1934*), Journeys and Places (*1937*), The Narrow Place (*1943*), The Voyage and Other Poems (*1946*). The Structure of the Novel (*1928*) *is a sound piece of criticism, and he has also written several novels.*

'The Wayside Station', a fine descriptive piece, is reprinted from The Narrow Place. *'The Combat,' not yet collected, is more typical of his art of metaphysical parable. Muir's earlier poetry was often involved and thin in texture, but since* Journeys and Places (*1937*) *the pressure of experience behind the gnomic element seems to have increased, and his latest poems are more interesting and memorable than the poems in his earlier books. There is an appreciative note on Muir's poetry in Stephen Spender's* Poetry Since 1939 (v. *Section VIII*).

The Wayside Station

Here at the wayside station, as many a morning,
I watch the smoke torn from the fumy engine
Crawling across the field in serpent sorrow.
Flat in the east, held down by stolid clouds,
The struggling day is born and shines already
On its warm hearth far off. Yet something here
Glimmers along the ground to show the seagulls
White on the furrows' black unturning waves.

But now the light has broadened.
I watch the farmstead on the little hill,
That seems to mutter: 'Here is day again'
Unwillingly. Now the sad cattle wake
In every byre and stall,
The ploughboy stirs in the loft, the farmer groans

And feels the day like a familiar ache
Deep in his body, though the house is dark.
The lovers part
Now in the bedroom where the pillows gleam
Great and mysterious as deep hills of snow,
An inaccessible land. The wood stands waiting
While the bright snare slips coil by coil around it,
Dark silver on every branch. The lonely stream
That rode through darkness leaps the gap of light,
Its voice grown loud, and starts its winding journey
Through the day and time and war and history.

The Combat

It was not meant for human eyes,
That combat on the shabby patch
Of clods and mangled grass that lies
Somewhere beneath the secret skies
For eye of toad or adder to catch.

And having seen it I accuse
The crested animal in his pride,
Arrayed in all those royal hues
Which hide the claws he well can use
To tear the heart out of the side.

Body of leopard, eagle's head
And whetted beak, and lion's mane,
And frost-grey hedge of feathers spread
Behind – he seemed of all things bred.
I shall not see his like again.

As for his enemy, there came in
A soft round beast as brown as clay;
All rent and patched his wretched skin;

A battered bag he might have been,
Some old used thing to throw away.

Yet he awaited face to face
The furious beast and the swift attack.
Soon over and done. That was no place
Or time for chivalry or for grace.
The fury had him on his back.

And two soft paws like hands flew out
To right and left while the trees stood by.
One would have said beyond a doubt
This was the very end of the bout,
But that the creature would not die.

For ere the death-blow he was gone,
Writhed, whirled, huddled into his den,
Safe somehow there. The fight was done,
And he had lost who had all but won.
But oh his deadly fury then.

A while the place lay bare, forlorn,
Drowsing as in relief from pain.
The cricket chirped, the grating thorn
Stirred, and a little sound was born.
The champions took their posts again.

And all began. The stealthy paw
Slashed out and in. Could nothing save
These rags and tatters from the claw?
Nothing. And yet I never saw
A beast so helpless and so brave.

And now, while the trees stand watching, still
The unequal battle rages there,
And the killing beast that cannot kill
Swells and swells in his fury till
You well might think it was despair.

T. S. ELIOT

Thomas Stearns Eliot was born of New England stock in St Louis, Missouri, in 1888, and educated at Harvard, Merton College, Oxford, and the Sorbonne. He settled in England in 1915 and became a naturalized British subject in 1927. After schoolmastering at Highgate – John Betjeman was a pupil – he was employed in the foreign department of Lloyds Bank in the City. In 1922 he founded The Criterion, *the best English literary review of its time, and soon after was appointed a Director of the publishing house of Faber and Faber, a post he still holds. The unequal* T. S. Eliot: a symposium (Editions Poetry London, 1948) *contains two contributions of great biographical interest: Wyndham Lewis on the 'Early London Environment' and F. V. Morley's 'T. S. Eliot as a Publisher'. The Order of Merit was bestowed on Mr Eliot in 1948, and his enormous influence on contemporary writing was also recognized by the award of the Nobel Prize for Literature. His other literary honours are too many to mention in full: he holds an honorary doctorate of many English and American universities, is an Honorary Fellow of Magdalene College, Cambridge, and has been Clark Lecturer at Cambridge (1926) and Charles Eliot Norton Visiting Professor at Harvard (1932–3). There is a bibliography of T. S. Eliot's writings by D. Gallup (Yale, 1947), but the ordinary reader or student will find enough in the useful check-list of published writings contained in* Focus Three: T. S. Eliot – a study of his writings by various hands.

T. S. Eliot's first volume of verse was Prufrock (1917). The Waste Land, *target for the arrows of the conventionally orthodox for many years, followed in 1922.* Collected Poems 1909–1935 (1936) *contains these and* Ash-Wednesday, *as well as shorter poems written before 1935.* Four Quartets – *the first part, 'Burnt Norton', appeared in* Collected Poems, *the other parts separately – was published in 1944. Other poetic works are the two verse plays,*

Murder in the Cathedral (*1935*) *and* The Family Reunion(*1939*), *and a book of verses for children,* Old Possum's Book of Practical Cats (*1939*). *Mr Eliot's latest play,* The Cocktail Party, *is not yet published, but it has been performed at the Edinburgh Festival (1949) and in New York (1950). Penguin Books have issued a useful* Selected Poems.

Apart from quite possibly being 'the greatest poetic influence in the world to-day' (Spender), T. S. Eliot is a literary critic of major importance, standing in relation to the present age much as Matthew Arnold (whom he sometimes, naturally enough, treats less than justly) did to the Victorian Age. As a critic he has modified the manner in which a whole generation regards 'the English poetic mind', and most of the shifts of emphasis in taste for which he has been responsible now seem with minor corrections natural and inevitable to students. The first critical essays and reviews were collected in The Sacred Wood (*1920*), *but the reader will now turn to* Selected Essays (*1932*) *for the critical work up to that date, and to later books such as* The Use of Poetry and The Use of Criticism (*1933*), After Strange Gods (*1934*), What is a Classic? (*1945*). The Idea of a Christian Society (*1939*) *and the recent* Notes towards the Definition of Culture (*1948*), *social criticism from a religious and cultural standpoint, should also be mentioned here. M. C. Bradbrook has written brightly on Eliot's literary criticism in* Focus Three.

Certain critical writings on T. S. Eliot's work have already been referred to. Attention should also be drawn to F. O. Mathiessen's The Achievement of T. S. Eliot, *first issued in 1935 and recently (1948) brought up to date; to R. Preston's* Four Quartets Rehearsed (*1946*); *and to H. Gardner's* The Art of T. S. Eliot (*1949*). *The vast amount of criticism in periodicals is beyond the scope of this note, and perhaps most of it can be safely neglected.*

The choice of poems from Mr Eliot's work to represent him in this anthology was limited by the fact that Four Quartets *is not available for reproduction. Originally I had intended to print the whole of the second movement from 'Little Gidding' instead of the extracts from* Murder in the Cathedral *and* The Family Reunion. *This movement, which begins with the lyric 'Ash on an Old Man's*

Sleeve' and develops into the superb rhetoric of the Dantesque inter-
view with 'the familiar compound ghost', seems to be Mr Eliot's
finest sustained passage of poetic writing, intense, grave, disciplined
and moving. It is, I think, unequalled by any other modern English
poet except Yeats. As with Yeats and Auden I feel dissatisfied with
my selection of poems – the work of all three poets is too various
for adequate representation even in the comparatively large amount
of space allotted to them.

Sweeney Erect

> And the trees about me,
> Let them be dry and leafless; let the rocks
> Groan with continual surges; and behind me,
> Make all a desolation. Look, look, wenches!

Paint me a cavernous waste shore
   Cast in the unstilled Cyclades,
Paint me the bold anfractuous rocks
   Faced by the snarled and yelping seas.

Display me Aeolus above
   Reviewing the insurgent gales
Which tangle Ariadne's hair
   And swell with haste the perjured sails.

Morning stirs the feet and hands
   (Nausicaa and Polypheme),
Gesture of orang-outang
   Rises from the sheets in steam.

This withered root of knots of hair
   Slitted below and gashed with eyes,
This oval O cropped out with teeth:
   The sickle motion from the thighs

Jackknifes upward at the knees
    Then straightens out from heel to hip
Pushing the framework of the bed
    And clawing at the pillow slip.

Sweeney addressed full length to shave
    Broadbottomed, pink from nape to base,
Knows the female temperament
    And wipes the suds around his face.

(The lengthened shadow of a man
    Is history, said Emerson
Who had not seen the silhouette
    Of Sweeney straddled in the sun.)

Tests the razor on his leg
    Waiting until the shriek subsides.
The epileptic on the bed
    Curves backward, clutching at her sides.

The ladies of the corridor
    Find themselves involved, disgraced,
Call witness to their principles
    And deprecate the lack of taste

Observing that hysteria
    Might easily be misunderstood;
Mrs Turner intimates
    It does the house no sort of good.

But Doris, towelled from the bath,
    Enters padding on broad feet,
Bringing sal volatile
    And a glass of brandy neat.

From *The Waste Land*

II. A Game of Chess

The Chair she sat in, like a burnished throne,
Glowed on the marble, where the glass
Held up by standards wrought with fruited vines
From which a golden Cupidon peeped out
(Another hid his eyes behind his wing)
Doubled the flames of sevenbranched candelabra
Reflecting light upon the table as
The glitter of her jewels rose to meet it,
From satin cases poured in rich profusion;
In vials of ivory and coloured glass
Unstoppered, lurked her strange synthetic perfumes,
Unguent, powdered, or liquid – troubled, confused
And drowned the sense in odours; stirred by the air
That freshened from the window, these ascended
In fattening the prolonged candle-flames,
Flung their smoke into the laquearia,
Stirring the pattern on the coffered ceiling.
Huge sea-wood fed with copper
Burned green and orange, framed by the coloured stone,
In which sad light a carvèd dolphin swam.
Above the antique mantel was displayed
As though a window gave upon the sylvan scene
The change of Philomel, by the barbarous king
So rudely forced; yet there the nightingale
Filled all the desert with inviolable voice
And still she cried, and still the world pursues,
'Jug Jug' to dirty ears.
And other withered stumps of time
Were told upon the walls; staring forms
Leaned out, leaning, hushing the room enclosed.
Footsteps shuffled on the stair.
Under the firelight, under the brush, her hair
Spread out in fiery points
Glowed into words, then would be savagely still.

'My nerves are bad to-night. Yes, bad. Stay with me.
'Speak to me. Why do you never speak. Speak.
     'What are you thinking of? What thinking? What?
'I never know what you are thinking. Think.'

I think we are in rats' alley
Where the dead men lost their bones.

'What is that noise?'
             The wind under the door.
'What is that noise now? What is the wind doing?'
          Nothing again nothing.
                       'Do
'You know nothing? Do you see nothing? Do you remember
'Nothing?'

    I remember
Those are pearls that were his eyes.
'Are you alive, or not? Is there nothing in your head?'

                                 But

O O O O that Shakespeherian Rag —
It's so elegant
So intelligent
'What shall I do now? What shall I do?'
'I shall rush out as I am, and walk the street
'With my hair down, so. What shall we do to-morrow?
'What shall we ever do?'
              The hot water at ten.
And if it rains, a closed car at four.
And we shall play a game of chess,
Pressing lidless eyes and waiting for a knock upon the door.

When Lil's husband got demobbed, I said —
I didn't mince my words, I said to her myself,
HURRY UP PLEASE ITS TIME

Now Albert's coming back, make yourself a bit smart.
He'll want to know what you done with that money he gave
    you
To get yourself some teeth. He did, I was there.
You have them all out, Lil, and get a nice set,
He said, I swear, I can't bear to look at you.
And no more can't I, I said, and think of poor Albert,
He's been in the army four years, he wants a good time.
And if you don't give it him, there's others will, I said.
Oh is there, she said. Something o' that, I said.
Then I'll know who to thank, she said, and give me a straight
    look.
HURRY UP PLEASE ITS TIME
If you don't like it you can get on with it, I said.
Others can pick and choose if you can't.
But if Albert makes off, it won't be for lack of telling.
You ought to be ashamed, I said, to look so antique.
(And her only thirty-one).
I can't help it, she said, pulling a long face,
It's them pills I took, to bring it off, she said.
(She's had five already, and nearly died of young George.)
The chemist said it would be all right, but I've never been the
    same.
You *are* a proper fool, I said.
Well, if Albert won't leave you alone, there it is, I said,
What you get married for if you don't want children?
HURRY UP PLEASE ITS TIME
Well, that Sunday Albert was home, they had a hot gammon,
And they asked me in to dinner, to get the beauty of it hot —
HURRY UP PLEASE ITS TIME
HURRY UP PLEASE ITS TIME
Goonight Bill. Goonight Lou. Goonight May. Goonight.
Ta ta. Goonight. Goonight.
Good night, ladies, good night, sweet ladies, good night, good
    night.

From *Ash-Wednesday*

VI

Although I do not hope to turn again
Although I do not hope
Although I do not hope to turn

Wavering between the profit and the loss
In this brief transit where the dreams cross
The dreamcrossed twilight between birth and dying
(Bless me father) though I do not wish to wish these things
From the wide window towards the granite shore
The white sails still fly seaward, seaward flying
Unbroken wings

And the lost heart stiffens and rejoices
In the lost lilac and the lost sea voices
And the weak spirit quickens to rebel
For the bent golden-rod and the lost sea smell
Quickens to recover
The cry of quail and the whirling plover
And the blind eye creates
The empty forms between the ivory gates
And smell renews the salt savour of the sandy earth

This is the time of tension between dying and birth
The place of solitude where three dreams cross
Between blue rocks
But when the voices shaken from the yew-tree drift away
Let the other yew be shaken and reply.

Blessèd sister, holy mother, spirit of the fountain, spirit of the
    garden,
Suffer us not to mock ourselves with falsehood
Teach us to care and not to care
Teach us to sit still

Even among these rocks,
Our peace in His will
And even among these rocks
Sister, mother
And spirit of the river, spirit of the sea,
Suffer me not to be separated

And let my cry come unto Thee.

From *Murder in the Cathedral*

Thomas soliloquizes

Now is my way clear, now is the meaning plain:
Temptation shall not come in this kind again.
The last temptation is the greatest treason:
To do the right deed for the wrong reason.
The natural vigour in the venial sin
Is the way in which our lives begin.
Thirty years ago, I searched all the ways
That lead to pleasure, advancement and praise.
Delight in sense, in learning and in thought,
Music and philosophy, curiosity,
The purple bullfinch in the lilac tree,
The tiltyard skill, the strategy of chess,
Love in the garden, singing to the instrument,
Were all things equally desirable.
Ambition comes when early force is spent
And when we find no longer all things possible.
Ambition comes behind and unobservable.
Sin grows with doing good. When I imposed the King's law
In England, and waged war with him against Toulouse,
I beat the barons at their own game. I
Could then despise the men who thought me most contemptible,
The raw nobility, whose manners matched their finger nails.
While I ate out of the King's dish

To become servant of God was never my wish.
Servant of God has chance of greater sin
And sorrow, than the man who serves a king.
For those who serve the greater cause may make the cause serve
    them,
Still doing right: and striving with political men
May make that cause political, not by what they do
But by what they are. I know
What yet remains to show you of my history
Will seem to most of you at best futility,
Senseless self-slaughter of a lunatic,
Arrogant passion of a fanatic.
I know that history at all time draws
The strangest consequence from remotest cause.
But for every evil, every sacrilege,
Crime, wrong, oppression and the axe's edge,
Indifference, exploitation, you, and you,
And you, must all be punished. So must you.
I shall no longer act or suffer, to the sword's end.
Now my good Angel, whom God appoints
To be my guardian, hover over the swords' points.

From *The Family Reunion*

Chorus

In an old house there is always listening, and more is heard than
    is spoken.
And what is spoken remains in the room, waiting for the future
    to hear it.
And whatever happens began in the past, and presses hard on
    the future.
The agony in the curtained bedroom, whether of birth or of
    dying,
Gathers in to itself all the voices of the past, and projects them
    into the future.

The treble voices on the lawn
The mowing of hay in summer
The dogs and the old pony
The stumble and the wail of little pain
The chopping of wood in autumn
And the singing in the kitchen
And the steps at night in the corridor
The moment of sudden loathing
And the season of stifled sorrow
The whisper, the transparent deception
The keeping up of appearances
The making the best of a bad job
All twined and tangled together, all are recorded.
There is no avoiding these things
And we know nothing of exorcism
And whether in Argos or England
There are certain inflexible laws
Unalterable, in the nature of music.
There is nothing at all to be done about it,
There is nothing to do about anything,
And now it is nearly time for the news
We must listen to the weather report
And the international catastrophes.

ARTHUR WALEY

Arthur Waley was born at Tunbridge Wells in 1889 and educated at Rugby and King's College, Cambridge (of which he is an Honorary Fellow). He was at one time Assistant Keeper of the Department of Prints and Drawings at the British Museum, and he worked in the Far Eastern section of the Ministry of Information during the Second World War. Among his publications are 170 Chinese Poems (*1918*), More Translations from the Chinese, The Nō Plays of Japan, The Tale of Genji, Monkey *and an*

Introduction to the Study of Chinese Painting. *The poems given here are from* Chinese Poems (*1946*), *a comprehensive selection from earlier volumes: both pieces are by Po Chü-i, of whom there is a short biographical notice in* 170 Chinese Poems, *and a new full-length biography by Mr Waley,* The Life and Times of Po Chü-i, 772–846 A.D. (*1950*). *The reader is also referred to* 170 Chinese Poems *for a valuable introduction to Chinese poetry and a note on the method of translation adopted. From this note I extract the following:*

> *I have aimed at literal translation, not paraphrase. It may be perfectly legitimate for a poet to borrow foreign themes or material, but this should not be called translation.*
>
> *Above all, considering imagery to be the soul of poetry, I have avoided either adding images of my own or suppressing those of the original.*
>
> *Any literal translation of Chinese poetry is bound to be to some extent rhythmical, for the rhythm of the original obtrudes itself. Translating literally, without thinking of the metre of the version, one finds that about two lines out of three have a very definite swing similar to that of the Chinese lines. The remaining lines are just too short or too long, a circumstance very irritating to the reader, whose ear expects the rhythm to continue. I have therefore tried to produce rhythmic effects similar to those of the original...I have not used rhyme...What is generally known as "blank verse" is the worst medium for translating Chinese poetry, because the essence of blank verse is that it varies the position of its pauses, whereas in Chinese the stop always comes at the end of the couplet.*

The Chrysanthemums in the Eastern Garden

(*Po Chü-i* A.D. 812)

The days of my youth left me long ago;
And now in their turn dwindle my years of prime.
With what thoughts of sadness and loneliness

I walk again in this cold, deserted place!
In the midst of the garden long I stand alone;
The sunshine, faint; the wind and dew chill.
The autumn lettuce is tangled and turned to seed;
The fair trees are blighted and withered away.
All that is left are a few chrysanthemum-flowers
That have newly opened beneath the wattled fence.
I had brought wine and meant to fill my cup,
When the sight of these made me stay my hand.
     I remember, when I was young,
How quickly my mood changed from sad to gay.
If I saw wine, no matter at what season,
Before I drank it, my heart was already glad.
       But now that age comes
A moment of joy is harder and harder to get.
And always I fear that when I am quite old
The strongest liquor will leave me comfortless.
Therefore I ask you, late chrysanthemum-flower,
At this sad season why do you bloom alone?
Though well I know that it was not for my sake,
Taught by you, for a while I will smooth my frown.

A Mad Poem addressed to my Nephews and Nieces

(Po Chü-i A.D. 835)

The World cheats those who cannot read;
I, happily, have mastered script and pen.
The World cheats those who hold no office;
I am blessed with high official rank.
Often the old have much sickness and pain;
With me, luckily, there is not much wrong.
People when they are old are often burdened with ties;
But *I* have finished with marriage and giving in marriage.
No changes happen to jar the quiet of my mind;
No business comes to impair the vigour of my limbs.

Hence it is that now for ten years
Body and soul have rested in hermit peace.
And all the more, in the last lingering years
What I shall need are very few things.
A single rug to warm me through the winter;
One meal to last me the whole day.
It does not matter that my house is rather small;
One cannot sleep in more than one room!
It does not matter that I have not many horses;
One cannot ride on two horses at once!
As fortunate as me among the people of the world
Possibly one would find seven out of ten.
As contented as me among a hundred men
Look as you may, you will not find one.
In the affairs of others even fools are wise;
In their own business even sages err.
To no one else would I dare to speak my heart.
So my wild words are addressed to my nephews and nieces.

ISAAC ROSENBERG

Isaac Rosenberg was born in Bristol in 1890. Seven years later his family moved to London and he went to an elementary school in London until he was fourteen, when he was apprenticed to an engraver. He was one of eight children and, while an apprentice, attended evening classes in art at Birkbeck College. Although he had written poetry from boyhood, he wanted to make painting his career and in 1911 he was able to enter the Slade School. In 1912 he published Night and Day, *the first of three pamphlets of poems, but neither these nor his paintings brought him any material success. He went to South Africa in 1914 in the hope of curing a weakness in his lungs. Returning to England in 1915, he enlisted in the Army and was killed in action in April, 1918. Gordon Bottomley edited his* Collected Poems (1922) — *this book contains a memoir by*

Laurence Binyon. The Collected Works (*poetry, letters, prose pieces*) *were published in 1937. The editors were Gordon Bottomley and Denys Harding, and there is a foreword by Siegfried Sassoon.*

'God Made Blind' is one of Rosenberg's earlier pieces and is printed in preference to the better-known war poems such as the much-anthologized 'Break of Day in the Trenches'. Rosenberg's poems show a talent for conceiving an idea in poetic terms and rendering it rhythmically, but they are spoilt for me by his appetite for the extravagant and his rebarbative poetic diction. 'He modelled words with fierce energy and aspiration,' says Sassoon: and again, 'his poetic visions are mostly in sombre colours and looming sculptural masses, molten and amply wrought.' Some critics have looked on him as a poet with promise of greatness — a view I cannot share; most critics are agreed that few of his actual poems are completely realized.

God Made Blind

It were a proud God-guiling, to allure
And flatter, by some cheat of ill, our Fate
To hold back the perfect crookedness its hate
Devised, and keep it poor,
And ignorant of our joy —
Masked in a giant wrong of cruel annoy,
That stands as some bleak hut to frost and night,
While hidden in bed is warmth and mad delight.

For all Love's heady valour and loved pain
Towers in our sinews that may not suppress
(Shut to God's eye) Love's springing eagerness,
And mind to advance his gain
Of gleeful secrecy
Through dolorous clay, which his eternity
Has pierced, in light that pushes out to meet
Eternity without us, heaven's heat.

And then, when Love's power hath increased so
That we must burst or grow to give it room,
And we can no more cheat our God with gloom,
We'll cheat Him with our joy.
For say! what can God do
To us, to Love, whom we have grown into?
Love! the poured rays of God's Eternity!
We are grown God – and shall His self-hate be?

RICHARD CHURCH

*Richard Church was born in London in 1873 and educated at
Dulwich Hamlet School. He was for twenty-four years a Civil
Servant – 'I loathed the bureaucratic machine, its capture by the
highly sterilized Fabian system, and all the backstair life of government and politics' – before becoming reader and literary adviser to
the publishing house of J. M. Dent & Sons. He has interested himself in verse-speaking and has been Examiner for Voice Production
and Verse Speaking at the University of London. With M. M.
Bozman he edited an anthology of contemporary verse for
Everyman's Library in 1945.*

*Richard Church is known both as a poet and a novelist. The best
of his novels is perhaps* The Porch *(1937), awarded the Femina Vie
Heureuse Prize for 1938. He has published more than a dozen books
of poetry · the earliest goes back to 1917 and two were published
during World War II,* The Solitary Man *and* A Twentieth
Century Psalter. *His* Collected Poems *(1948) reveal that his
talent is happiest in reflecting on personal experience. He is not a
poet whose work shows originality of theme or intensity of emotion,
but he has the virtues which result from a respect for craftsmanship – even if that term is narrowly conceived – and a refusal to
attempt what is outside his range.*

From *The Lamp*

Now all things are changing, earth
Destroys itself in a new birth.
Mountains, as was prophesied,
Vanish, and the seas have dried.
Corn is withered, and no green
Leaf upon the tree is seen.
Silent, lifeless in light's glare
The moon-scape of the world lies bare.

Time runs down, and as it ceases,
Star-denuded space releases
All that has been, all that is,
All our future histories.
In this break of logic's chain
Cause and effect no more remain
Dictators of our destiny.

The mathematics of the sky
Lose their cog-wheeled potency,
And incalculable slumber
Seals the eye of godlike Number;
Godlike, but not yet the son
Of the shell-borne beauty blown
Out of spindrift, out of foam
To the soul of man, her home.

Now the moment comes for all
Religions' final festival;
The trial, the torture, the last breath
Of God in man, the deathless death;
The sojourn in the sepulchre;
The miracle of bones that stir
Within the cerecloth; the great stone
Rolled back, and one who walks alone
Still faithful through this dark and damp
Solstice of life, bearing a lamp.

HERBERT READ

Herbert Read was born in Yorkshire in 1893, the son of a farmer, and was studying at Leeds University when the first World War began. He served as an infantry officer in France and Belgium and was awarded the D.S.O. and M.C. After the war he held various posts in the Civil Service, including a ten-year period in the Victoria and Albert Museum, South Kensington, where he specialized in ceramics and stained glass, before becoming Watson Gordon Professor of Fine Art at Edinburgh University. From 1933 to 1939 he was editor of The Burlington Magazine, *and in 1937 he became a director of the joint publishing firms of Kegan Paul and George Routledge. He has been Clark Lecturer at Cambridge and Sydney Jones Lecturer in Art at Liverpool University; and he holds an Honorary D.Litt. of Leeds University. He is also an Hon. Fellow of the Society of Industrial Artists.*

Herbert Read is a very prolific writer and apart from fiction (The Green Child) *and autobiography* (Annals of Innocence and Experience) *has written on aesthetics, literature, the history of art, education, politics and sociology. Some idea of his varied interests and the intelligence he brings to bear on them can be obtained by looking at* Herbert Read: an Introduction to his Work by Various Hands, *edited by Henry Treece, or by turning the pages of such collections of essays, lectures and reviews as* The Politics of the Unpolitical (1943) *or* A Coat of Many Colours (1945). *Among his best books on literature in my opinion are* English Prose Style (1928), Wordsworth (1930) *and* Poetry and Anarchism (1938). *He is a pioneer in the field of industrial art, and his* The Meaning of Art (1931), Art Now (1933), Art and Society (1936) *and* Education Through Art (1943) *have done something to make the educable public less Philistine about the visual arts.*

Collected Poems (1946) *supersedes the earlier collection,* Poems 1914–1934. *A favourable judgment is given of his poetry by Edwin*

Muir in The Present Age (*'Introductions to English Literature'*, *Vol. V*), *but I find myself agreeing with Stephen Spender, who points out that Mr Read's verse lacks inevitability and that 'one feels he has worked hard to say something which might have been as well differently said'. In my view only a fraction of his intelligence and erudition penetrates his verse, and the comparatively small harvest of it contains much which a stricter self-discipline would have removed (e.g. 'Picaresque' – an obvious bit of E. E. Cummings – and most of the 'Eclogues,' Imagist fragments which have not worn well).*

'Sedate within this palisade' is the second part of 'A World Within a War' from the section 'War Poems (1936–45)' in Collected Poems.

A World within a War

II

Sedate within this palisade
Which unforethinking I have made

Of brittle leaves and velvet flowers,
I re-indite a Book of Hours –

Would emulate the Lombard School
(Crisp as medals, bright but cool)

Talk mainly of the Human Passion
That made us in a conscious fashion

Strive to control our human fate:
But in the margins interpolate

Apes and angels playing tunes
On harpsichords or saxophones

Throughout the story thus maintain
Under a sacred melody the bass profane.

My saints were often silly men
Fond of wine and loose with women.

When they rose to holy stature
They kept the whims of human nature

Were mystics in their London gardens
Or wore instead of hairshirts burdens

Of a mild domestic sort: but so devout
That suddenly they would go out

And die for freedom in the street
Or fall like partridges before a butt

Of ambush'd tyranny and hate.
Other legends will relate

The tale of men whose only love
Was simple work: whose usual lives

Were formed in mirth and music, or in words
Whose golden echoes are wild rewards

For all our suffering, unto death...

On the last page a colophon
Would conclude the liberal plan

Showing Man within a frame
Of trophies stolen from a dream.

WILFRED OWEN

Wilfred Owen was born at Plas Wilmot, Oswestry, in 1893 and educated at the Birkenhead Institute and the University of London. He began writing verse in 1910 and was encouraged by the friendship of the French poet, Laurent Tailhade, whom he met when he went to Bordeaux after an illness to become a tutor. In 1915 he enlisted in the Artists' Rifles and was gazetted to the Manchester Regiment. After the Somme battles in 1917 he was invalided home and was sent to the Craiglockhart War Hospital, where he was happy composing poetry, lecturing and making friends (v. notice of Sassoon above). He returned to his regiment in 1918, and, after being awarded the M.C., was killed by machine-gun fire at the crossing of the Sambre Canal on November 4, 1918. His poems were collected by Siegfried Sassoon and published in 1920. The much fuller The Poems of Wilfred Owen *(1933) was edited with a memoir and notes by Edmund Blunden. A complete edition of Owen's poems (including juvenilia) and an edition of the letters are badly needed.*

Wilfred Owen was the most important of the 'war-poets' of World War I and his poetic endowment as revealed in his published work allows us to think of him as potentially a great poet. He certainly had the intelligence and the artistic integrity, and he was able to experiment vitally in technical matters — he was, says Blunden, 'an unwearied worker in the laboratory of word, rhythm, and music of language'. His discovery of the para-rhyme — and use of it in the war-poems to create 'remoteness, darkness, emptiness, shock' — was an invention of a very important order, and its subsequent too indiscriminate use by poets of the 'thirties should not blind us to this fact. (But see Auden's Poems 1930, III, *for an intelligent employment of para-rhyme.) The peculiar power of Owen's poetry seems to me to spring from the sudden maturity forced by war experience on a naturally rich, Keatsian sensibility. 'My senses are charred,' he wrote, 'I don't take the cigarette out of my mouth when*

I write Deceased over their letters.' The final comment on his poems ought to be his own. He had been planning a book of poems just before he was killed, and rough drafts of a Preface and Contents found among his papers are given in Blunden's sensitive memoir. The following is from the Preface:

> *This book is not about heroes. English poetry is not yet fit to speak of them.*
> *Nor is it about deeds, or lands, nor anything about glory, honour, might, majesty, dominion, or power, except War.*
> *Above all I am not concerned with Poetry.*
> *My subject is War, and the pity of War.*
> *The Poetry is in the pity.*
> *Yet these elegies are to this generation in no sense consolatory. They may be to the next. All a poet can do to-day is warn. That is why the true Poets must be truthful.*

'Strange Meeting', given here, is often spoken of as Wilfred Owen's masterpiece, but I find 'Insensibility' the most satisfying of his poems.

Exposure

Our brains ache, in the merciless iced east winds that knive us...
Wearied we keep awake because the night is silent...
Low, drooping flares confuse our memory of the salient...
Worried by silence, sentries whisper, curious, nervous,
      But nothing happens.

Watching, we hear the mad gusts tugging on the wire,
Like twitching agonies of men among its brambles.
Northward, incessantly, the flickering gunnery rumbles,
Far off, like a dull rumour of some other war.
      What are we doing here?

The poignant misery of dawn begins to grow...
We only know war lasts, rain soaks, and clouds sag stormy.
Dawn massing in the east her melancholy army
Attacks once more in ranks on shivering ranks of gray,
      But nothing happens.

Sudden successive flights of bullets streak the silence.
Less deadly than the air that shudders black with snow,
With sidelong flowing flakes that flock, pause, and renew,
We watch them wandering up and down the wind's nonchalance
      But nothing happens.

Pale flakes with fingering stealth come feeling for our faces –
We cringe in holes, back on forgotten dreams, and stare, snow-
    dazed,
Deep into grassier ditches. So we drowse, sun-dozed,
Littered with blossoms trickling where the blackbird fusses.
      Is it that we are dying?

Slowly our ghosts drag home: glimpsing the sunk fires, glozed
With crusted dark-red jewels; crickets jingle there;
For hours the innocent mice rejoice: the house is theirs;
Shutters and doors, all closed: on us the doors are closed, –
      We turn back to our dying.

Since we believe not otherwise can kind fires burn;
Nor ever suns smile true on child, or field, or fruit.
For God's invincible spring our love is made afraid;
Therefore, not loath, we lie out here; therefore were born,
      For love of God seems dying.

To-night, His frost will fasten on this mud and us,
Shrivelling many hands, puckering foreheads crisp.
The burying-party, picks and shovels in their shaking grasp,
Pause over half-known faces. All their eyes are ice,
      But nothing happens.

Insensibility

I

Happy are men who yet before they are killed
Can let their veins run cold.
Whom no compassion fleers
Or makes their feet
Sore on the alleys cobbled with their brothers.
The front line withers,
But they are troops who fade, not flowers
For poets' tearful fooling:
Men, gaps for filling:
Losses who might have fought
Longer; but no one bothers.

II

And some cease feeling
Even themselves or for themselves.
Dullness best solves
The tease and doubt of shelling,
And Chance's strange arithmetic
Comes simpler than the reckoning of their shilling.
They keep no check on armies' decimation.

III

Happy are these who lose imagination:
They have enough to carry with ammunition.
Their spirit drags no pack,
Their old wounds save with cold can not more ache.
Having seen all things red,
Their eyes are rid
Of the hurt of the colour of blood for ever.
And terror's first constriction over,
Their hearts remain small-drawn.
Their senses in some scorching cautery of battle
Now long since ironed,
Can laugh among the dying, unconcerned.

IV

Happy the soldier home, with not a notion
How somewhere, every dawn, some men attack,
And many sighs are drained.
Happy the lad whose mind was never trained:
His days are worth forgetting more than not.
He sings along the march
Which we march taciturn, because of dusk,
The long, forlorn, relentless trend
From larger day to huger night.

V

We wise, who with a thought besmirch
Blood over all our soul,
How should we see our task
But through his blunt and lashless eyes?
Alive, he is not vital overmuch;
Dying, not mortal overmuch;
Nor sad, nor proud,
Nor curious at all.
He cannot tell
Old men's placidity from his.

VI

But cursed are dullards whom no cannon stuns,
That they should be as stones;
Wretched are they, and mean
With paucity that never was simplicity.
By choice they made themselves immune
To pity and whatever moans in man
Before the last sea and the hapless stars;
Whatever mourns when many leave these shores;
Whatever shares
The eternal reciprocity of tears.

Strange Meeting

It seemed that out of battle I escaped
Down some profound dull tunnel, long since scooped
Through granites which titanic wars had groined.
Yet also there encumbered sleepers groaned,
Too fast in thought or death to be bestirred.
Then, as I probed them, one sprang up, and stared
With piteous recognition in fixed eyes,
Lifting distressful hands as if to bless.
And by his smile, I knew that sullen hall,
By his dead smile I knew we stood in Hell.
With a thousand pains that vision's face was grained;
Yet no blood reached there from the upper ground,
And no guns thumped, or down the flues made moan.
'Strange friend,' I said, 'here is no cause to mourn.'
'None,' said the other, 'save the undone years,
The hopelessness. Whatever hope is yours,
Was my life also; I went hunting wild
After the wildest beauty in the world,
Which lies not calm in eyes, or braided hair,
But mocks the steady running of the hour,
And if it grieves, grieves richlier than here.
For by my glee might many men have laughed,
And of my weeping something had been left,
Which must die now. I mean the truth untold,
The pity of war, the pity war distilled.
Now men will go content with what we spoiled.
Or, discontent, boil bloody, and be spilled.
They will be swift with swiftness of the tigress,
None will break ranks, though nations trek from progress.
Courage was mine, and I had mystery,
Wisdom was mine, and I had mastery;
To miss the march of this retreating world
Into vain citadels that are not walled.
Then, when much blood had clogged their chariot-wheels

I would go up and wash them from sweet wells,
Even with truths that lie too deep for taint.
I would have poured my spirit without stint
But not through wounds; not on the cess of war.
Foreheads of men have bled where no wounds were.
I am the enemy you killed, my friend.
I knew you in this dark; for so you frowned
Yesterday through me as you jabbed and killed.
I parried; but my hands were loath and cold.
Let us sleep now ... '

ALDOUS HUXLEY

Aldous Huxley was born in July, 1894, the third son of Leonard Huxley and grandson of the Victorian scientist. He was educated at Eton and Balliol College, Oxford – the process being interrupted by disease of the eyes – and then worked in London for some years as a journalist and dramatic critic. Since that time he has devoted himself entirely to writing, living first on the Continent and then in California (where he moved in the 'thirties). He has published nearly forty books: novels, poems, plays, travel, biography and philosophy. A standard collected edition is now being issued.

Aldous Huxley is an extraordinarily well-read, intelligent and – up to a point – psychologically perceptive commentator on books, ideas and people, but it is a question whether he has ever written a good novel, and there is no question at all about his rank as a poet: he is not a poet, but a writer of verses – and the best of these are the lightest and most frivolous. The title-poem of Leda *(1920) is now painful·to read for the gaucherie of its 'teen-age sensuality. The two songs here given are from this volume and are good examples of nose-thumbing undergraduate wit. They are included because they seem to me to tell us something about one side of the 'twenties, and because they furnish a piquant, if ribald, comment on the Mr Huxley of* The Perennial Philosophy *(1946).*

Second Philosopher's Song

If, O my Lesbia, I should commit,
Not fornication, dear, but suicide,
My Thames-blown body (Pliny vouches it)
Would drift face upwards on the oily tide
With the other garbage, till it putrefied.

But you; if all your lovers' frozen hearts
Conspired to send you, desperate, to drown –
Your maiden modesty would float face down,
And men would weep upon your hinder parts.

'Tis the Lord's doing. Marvellous is the plan
By which this best of worlds is wisely planned.
One law he made for woman, one for man:
We bow the head and do not understand.

Fifth Philosophers' Song

A million million spermatozoa,
    All of them alive:
Out of their cataclysm but one poor Noah
    Dare hope to survive.

And among that billion minus one
    Might have chanced to be
Shakespeare, another Newton, a new Donne –
    But the One was Me.

Shame to have ousted your betters thus,
    Taking ark while the others remained outside!
Better for all of us, froward Homunculus,
    If you'd quietly died!

ROBERT GRAVES

Robert Graves was born in London in 1895 of mixed 'Irish-Scottish-Danish-German' parentage. He was educated at Charterhouse and St John's College, Oxford. During World War I he served with the Royal Welch Fusiliers in France and was officially reported 'Died of Wounds' on his twenty-first birthday. He survived to read English Language and Literature at Oxford and to become (for one year) Professor of English Literature at Cairo on the recommendation of T. E. Lawrence. Goodbye To All That (*1929*) *is an autobiographical account of this phase of his life: it is an exceptionally truthful, interesting and well-written book. Since that time Graves has lived by writing.*

During the 'thirties he worked in Majorca where (in association with Laura Riding) he ran the Seizin Press, publishing a number of books and the critical miscellany, Epilogue. *He returned to England during the Spanish Civil War and lived in this country (except for short periods in France and America) until his recent return to Majorca.*

He is probably best known by the ordinary reading public for his historical novels: I, Claudius (*1934*), *for which he was awarded the Hawthornden Prize and the James Tait Black Prize, and its sequel,* Claudius the God (*1934*); Count Belisarius (*1938*); Wife to Mr Milton (*1943*); The Golden Fleece (*1944*); King Jesus (*1946*), *etc. But he has also published a good deal of criticism, including the admirable* On English Poetry (*1922*), *and the recent collection of essays,* The Common Asphodel (*1949*). The White Goddess (*1948*) *for its erudite 'mélange adultère de tout' and its unflinching statement of his insight into the nature of poetic experience will madden the conventional.*

The bibliography of his poems is sure to provide headaches for future scholars. Collected Poems (*1938*) *draws on nineteen earlier volumes, but omits a great deal of good work — 'whatever I felt misrepresented my poetic seriousness at the time when it was written'. This collection contains a Foreword in which the poet describes his own poetic development: 'I should say that my health as a poet lies in my mistrust of the comfortable point-of-rest.' Since 1938 he has produced* Work in Hand *(1942), with Alan Hodge and Norman Cameron, and* Poems 1938–1945 *(1945). In 1948 a revised edition of* Collected Poems *was issued.*

The poetry of Robert Graves is in some ways the purest poetry produced in our time, waving no flags, addressed to no congregations, designed neither to comfort nor persuade. It is poetry rooted in everyday experience, but it always has the quality of making that experience new, pungent and exciting. Of the poems included in this anthology 'Welsh Incident' is the lightest. I choose it because it is very funny and written with great skill. 'Warning to Children' and 'Lollocks' are small, perfectly acceptable examples of myth-making. 'Never Such Love' and 'The Thieves' are love-poems of a sort too truthful for the many to admire without misgiving. What, finally, I observe and admire in Graves – and in hardly any other poet in this anthology (except Yeats) is it found so purely – is the acceptance of his poetic vocation and his single-minded devotion to it as a way of life.

Warning to Children

Children, if you dare to think
Of the greatness, rareness, muchness,
Fewness of this precious only
Endless world in which you say
You live, you think of things like this:
Blocks of slate enclosing dappled
Red and green, enclosing tawny
Yellow nets, enclosing white
And black acres of dominoes,
Where a neat brown paper parcel
Tempts you to untie the string.

In the parcel a small island,
On the island a large tree,
On the tree a husky fruit.
Strip the husk and cut the rind off:
In the centre you will see
Blocks of slate enclosed by dappled
Red and green, enclosed by tawny
Yellow nets, enclosed by white
And black acres of dominoes,
Where the same brown paper parcel –
Children, leave the string untied!
For who dares undo the parcel
Finds himself at once inside it,
On the island, in the fruit,
Blocks of slate about his head,
Finds himself enclosed by dappled
Green and red, enclosed by yellow
Tawny nets, enclosed by black
And white acres of dominoes,
But the same brown paper parcel
Still untied upon his knee.
And, if he then should dare to think
Of the fewness, muchness, rareness,
Greatness of this endless only
Precious world in which he says
He lives – he then unties the string.

Welsh Incident

'But that was nothing to what things came out
From the sea-caves of Criccieth yonder.'
'What were they? Mermaids? dragons? ghosts?'
'Nothing at all of any things like that.'
'What were they, then?'
                          'All sorts of queer things,

Things never seen or heard or written about,
Very strange, un-Welsh, utterly peculiar
Things. Oh, solid enough they seemed to touch,
Had anyone dared it. Marvellous creation,
All various shapes and sizes and no sizes,
All new, each perfectly unlike his neighbour,
Though all came moving slowly out together.'
'Describe just one of them.'
                                    'I am unable.'
'What were their colours?'
                                    'Mostly nameless colours,
Colours you'd like to see; but one was puce
Or perhaps more like crimson, but not purplish.
Some had no colour.'
                                    'Tell me, had they legs?'
'Not a leg or foot among them that I saw.'
'But did these things come out in any order?
What o'clock was it? What was the day of the week?
Who else was present? What was the weather?'
'I was coming to that. It was half-past three
On Easter Tuesday last. The sun was shining.
The Harlech Silver Band played *Marchog Jesu*
On thirty-seven shimmering instruments,
Collecting for Carnarvon's (Fever) Hospital Fund.
The populations of Pwllheli, Criccieth,
Portmadoc, Borth, Tremadoc, Penrhyndeudraeth,
Were all assembled. Criccieth's mayor addressed them
First in good Welsh and then in fluent English,
Twisting his fingers in his chain of office,
Welcoming the things. They came out on the sand,
Not keeping time to the band, moving seaward
Silently at a snail's pace. But at last
The most odd, indescribable thing of all
Which hardly one man there could see for wonder
Did something recognizably a something.'
'Well, what?'
                                    'It made a noise.'

'A frightening noise?'
'No, no.'
   'A musical noise? A noise of scuffling?'
'No, but a very loud, respectable noise –
Like groaning to oneself on Sunday morning
In Chapel, close before the second psalm.'
'What did the mayor do?'
     'I was coming to that.'

Never Such Love

Twined together and, as is customary,
For words of rapture groping, they
'Never such love,' swore, 'ever before was!'
Contrast with all loves that had failed or staled
Registered their own as love indeed.

And was this not to blab idly
The heart's fated inconstancy?
Better in love to seal the love-sure lips:
For truly love was before words were,
And no word given, no word broken.

When the name 'love' is uttered
(Love, the near-honourable malady
With which in greed and haste they
Each other do infect and curse)
Or, worse, is written down ...

Wise after the event, by love withered,
A 'never more!' most frantically
Sorrow and shame would proclaim
Such as, they'd swear, never before were:
True lovers even in this.

Lollocks

By sloth on sorrow fathered,
These dusty-featured Lollocks
Have their nativity in all disordered
Backs of cupboard drawers.

They play hide and seek
Among collars and novels
And empty medicine bottles,
And letters from abroad
That never will be answered.

Every sultry night
They plague little children,
Gurgling from the cistern,
Humming from the air,
Skewing up the bed-clothes,
Twitching the blind.

When the imbecile agèd
Are over-long in dying
And the nurse drowses,
Lollocks come skipping
Up the tattered stairs
And are nasty together
In the bed's shadow.

The signs of their presence
Are boils on the neck,
Dreams of vexation suddenly recalled
In the middle of the morning,
Languor after food.

Men cannot see them,
Men cannot hear them,

Do not believe in them –
But suffer the more,
Both in neck and belly.

Women can see them –
O those naughty wives
Who sit by the fireside
Munching bread and honey,
Watching them in mischief
From corners of their eyes,
Slily allowing them to lick
Honey-sticky fingers.

Sovereign against Lollocks,
Are hard broom and soft broom,
To well comb the hair,
To well brush the shoe,
And to pay every debt
So soon as it's due.

The Thieves

Lovers in the act dispense
With such meum-tuum sense
As might warningly reveal
What they must not pick or steal,
And their nostrum is to say:
'I and you are both away'.

After when they disentwine
You from me and yours from mine,
Neither can be certain who
Was that I whose mine was you.
To the act again they go
More completely not to know.

Theft is theft and raid is raid
Though reciprocally made.
Lovers, the conclusion is
Doubled sighs and jealousies
In a single heart that grieves
For lost honour among thieves.

EDMUND BLUNDEN

*Edmund Blunden writes as follows: 'I was born in 1896, educated
at Christ's Hospital and published my first little books there,
served with the Royal Sussex Regiment from 1915 to 1919 [he was
awarded the M.C.], and after a few terms at Oxford became a
miscellaneous writer. In Japan, where I taught English Literature
at Tokyo University from 1924 to 1927, I wrote* Undertones of
War, *which may be my best production. From 1931 to 1944 I was
Fellow of Merton College, Oxford, and sometime Sub-Warden.
My last book of poems was* Shells by a Stream (1944). *I am at the
moment* [1948] *in Japan again, appointed a member of the U.K.
Liaison Mission; lecturing to many universities and schools.' This
concise account omits the awards of the Hawthornden Prize in 1922
and of the Benson Medal of the Royal Society of Literature in
1930, and does not mention Mr Blunden's biographical studies of
Leigh Hunt, Charles Lamb, John Taylor (publisher of Keats) and
Shelley.* Poems 1914–1930 (1930), Poems 1930–1940 (1940),
Shells by a Stream (1944) *and* After the Bombing (1949) *span
his poetic production, each of the two collected editions containing
the substance of several earlier volumes.*

'The Pike' *and* 'The Midnight Skaters' *are reprinted from*
Poems 1914-1930 *and* 'October Comes' *from* Shells by a Stream.

*Mr Blunden has at times been lumped with the Georgians, but
one has to observe how the attempt to 'compose' a pastoral world –*

*sometimes even by echoes and imitations of Augustan pastoralists
and by seeing landscapes not directly but through an artist's eyes –
and the exquisite delicacy and formality of movement in many
poems imply a criticism of a merely naïve direct approach to the
writing of nature-poetry: and to notice how this separates him from
the ordinary Georgian poet. I particularly appreciate in Blunden
the niceness of the observation – sometimes it is finical – and the
subtle way human unease is hinted at in much verse which at first
would appear to be purely descriptive. 'October Comes', with its
haunting ominous lightness of rhythm and its near-archaisms in
diction, illustrates some of these points well.*

The Pike

From shadows of rich oaks outpeer
The moss-green bastions of the weir,
Where the quick dipper forages
In elver-peopled crevices,
And a small runlet trickling down the sluice
Gossamer music tires not to unloose.

Else round the broad pool's hush
Nothing stirs,
Unless sometimes a straggling heifer crush
Through the thronged spinney where the pheasant whirs
Or martins in a flash
Come with wild mirth to dip their magical wings,
While in the shallow some doomed bulrush swings
At whose hid root the diver vole's teeth gnash.

And nigh this toppling reed, still as the dead
The great pike lies, the murderous patriarch
Watching the waterpit sheer-shelving dark,
Where through the plash his lithe bright vassals thread.

The rose-finned roach and bluish bream
And staring ruffe steal up the stream
Hard by their glutted tyrant, now
Still as a sunken bough.

He on the sandbank lies,
    Sunning himself long hours
With stony gorgon eyes:
    Westward the hot sun lowers.

Sudden the gray pike changes, and quivering poises for
    slaughter;
        Intense terror wakens around him, the shoals scud
            awry, but there chances
        A chub unsuspecting; the prowling fins quicken, in
            fury he lances;
And the miller that opens the hatch stands amazed at the whirl
    in the water.

The Midnight Skaters

The hop-poles stand in cones,
    The icy pond lurks under,
The pole-tops steeple to the thrones
    Of stars, sound gulfs of wonder;
But not the tallest there, 'tis said,
Could fathom to this pond's black bed.

Then is not death at watch
    Within those secret waters?
What wants he but to catch
    Earth's heedless sons and daughters?
With but a crystal parapet
Between, he has his engines set.

Then on, blood shouts, on, on,
   Twirl, wheel and whip above him,
Dance on this ball-floor thin and wan,
   Use him as though you love him;
Court him, elude him, reel and pass,
And let him hate you through the glass.

October Comes

I heard the graybird bathing in the rill,
And fluttering his wings dry within thorn boughs
Which all embowered the rill; with tiny bill
The robin on red-berried spray bade rouse
    One whom I could not see, a field away;
    I heard the passing girl to her young man say,
'O look, there's a buttercup'; for Autumn brought them still.

Upon my hand the fly so small that sight
Hardly could shape him settled, quested, flew;
Above me crowns of cloud and thrones of light
Moved with the minutes, and the season's blue,
    Autumn's soft raiment, veiled some forms of dream
    Which I yet reverence; once more to my stream
The clear forget-me-not drew my eyes; the vole watched too.

He watched, and ate his chosen leaf; well-furred,
Well-fed he felt for water, winter, all.
Whoever else came by, midge, moth or bird,
The time was easy, nor did one leaf fall
    From willow or elm that hour, though millions
      glowed
    With such wild flame as evening shot abroad
To warn that even this calm was not perpetual.

SACHEVERELL SITWELL

Sacheverell Sitwell, younger brother of Osbert and Edith Sitwell, was born at Scarborough in 1897, and educated at Eton and Balliol College, Oxford. He has published a biography of Liszt, studies of Mozart and of baroque art – of these Southern Baroque Art *(1924) is often held to be the best – as well as much imaginative miscellaneous prose typified by such a book as* Primitive Scenes and Festivals *(1943). He has also written many volumes of poetry and a piece of semi-autobiographical fiction,* All Summer in a Day *(1926). Among the collections of verse are* Doctor Donne and Gargantua *(1930),* Canons of Giant Art *(1933) and* Dance of the Quick and the Dead *(1936). A useful volume of* Selected Poems, *with a preface by Osbert Sitwell, was issued in 1948.*

Selected Poems *reveals the completeness of the poet's creation of a lyrical 'aesthetic' world in which he is at home, and his perpetual concern for the kind of craftsmanship needed to release his imaginative vision.*

The two contrasted passages of description and reflection by which Mr Sitwell is represented here are taken from Canons of Giant Art, *which is, I think, his best collection of poetry.*

From *Upon an Image from Dante*

Clouds touched the church-towers
The streets were spray
A hundred feet in the air and all the world was waste
A hundred feet to sea and there was nothing living
Nothing but waves and the cauldron of the rocks:
So near the edge
In warm rooms and in the lamp-lit streets,
With a cab-horse trotting past the stuccoed houses

And the gale at the corner, that November night:
In the month of thunder, in the noise of timber
I was born in November by the stormy sea,
So near death to be born into the living,
Nearer than the rich man to the millions starving.

And the winter went, and many other winters,
And we walked by the sea's edge to Cornelian bay,
By a shore of wreckage, of the sundered timbers,
Finding dark jet and the wonders of the ammonite:
All there was of men was the smoke above their houses
Below the green baize cliff, up to the ruined castle,
Giving on the harbour, on the masted shipping.
So was all their coast, to Whitby and beyond,
A land of little harbours, little stilt-like houses
Standing in the tides;
Sometimes a doorway of the jawbones of a whale,
A netted anchor, or the figure from a ship,
Dredged from the seas, stood in a white-washed yard
For spoil from the shoals, from shimmer of the mackerel:
And the year went in wonders, the great spring-tide
Ebbed with the moon, in an electric morning
When air sparkled and flashed, when all the world was new;
That tide left the harbour dry; the keel-less ships
Leaned to one side, toppling on the sand;
It ebbed at another shore, far down the sea,
Laid bare for this, refulgent with new light
On rocks, not seen before, new islands in the plain
Glittering with pools, the little fronded seas
Where waved green weeds or dryed their greener tresses
On mermaid rocks and crackled in their pods,
Instinct with iodine. The archipelago
Glistened, all shining, new-risen from the sea:
The salt airs out upon those frontiers
Were the breath of Creation till the spring-tide flowed
When the isles sank and vanished, and the leaning vessels
Righted their keels: the high tide, towering,

Took new sands and piled against the piers
Swollen in fury, as in a race of waters,
All, all for nothing, for one morning of the spring.

From *Agamemnon's Tomb*

The poor are fast forgotten,
They outnumber the living, but where are all their bones?
For every man alive there are a million dead,
Has their dust gone into earth that it is never seen?
There should be no air to breathe, with it so thick,
No space for wind to blow, nor rain to fall;
Earth should be a cloud of dust, a soil of bones,
With no room, even, for our skeletons;
It is wasted time to think of it, to count its grains,
When all are alike and there's no difference in them;
They wait in the dark corridors, in earth's black galleries,
But the doors never open; they are dead, dead, dead.
Ah! Seek not the difference in king or beggar:
The King has his gold with him, that will not buy,
It is better to have starved and to be used to it.
Is there no comfort down the long dead years,
No warmth in prison, no love left for dead bones;
Does no one come to kiss them? Answer, none, none, none.
Yet that was their longing, to be held and given,
To be handed to death while held in arms that loved them,
For his greater care, who saw that they were loved
And would take note of it and favour them in prison;
But, instead, he stood more near to them, his chill was in them,
And the living were warm, the last of love was warm;
Oh! One more ray of it, one beam before the winter,
Before they were unborn, beyond the blind, unborn,
More blind and puny, carried back into the dark,

But without rumour, with no fate to come,
Nothing but waiting, waiting long for nothing.

It was too late to weep, this was the last of time,
The light flickered, but tears would dim it more:
It was better to be calm and keep the taste of life;
But a sip or two of life, and then, forever, death.
Oh! The cold, the sinking cold, the falling from the edge
Where love was no help and could not hold one back,
Falling, falling, falling into blackest dark,
Falling while hands touched one, while the lips felt warm,
If one was loved, and was not left alone.

Now it was so little that a babe was more,
No more of self, a little feeble thing
That love could not help,
That none could love for what it was;
It looked, and love saw it, but it could not answer:
Life's mystery was finished, only death was clear,
It was sorry for the living, it was glad to die,
Death was its master, it belonged to death.

O kiss it no more, it is so cold and pale,
It is not of this world, it is no part of us;
Not the soul we loved, but something pitiful
The hands should not touch. Oh! Leave it where it lies;
Let the dead where they die; come out among the living;
Weep not over dead bones; your tears are wasted.

ROY CAMPBELL

*Roy Campbell writes: 'I was born in October 1901, and brought up
in the Union and Southern Rhodesia. I joined the 6th South African
Infantry when I was fifteen. I came to Europe in 1919 and have
made three trips back home since then, two of them being on leave
during this last war. I have lived most of my adult life in Spain,
Portugal and France – mostly in the horse-line. I fought in the
Spanish War and this last war as a volunteer. I volunteered for the
British Army on September 3rd, 1939, but, as I was over age and a
South African subject, they wouldn't accept me till over a year
afterwards. I did my Infantry training with the Royal Welch
Fusiliers and the South Wales Borderers at Brecon. I served in
East and North Africa and ended up as a Sergeant in one of the
East African Reception Units, a crack fighting unit, which went to
Burma. I was permanently disabled during training, with a broken
hip joint, and discharged with a life pension after a year in hospital
and convalescent camps. Being permanently crippled I had to take a
sedentary job as a clerk. There is no more horse-breaking or bull-
fighting for me. So I am now almost naturalized a Cockney of
London Town.'*

Among his publications the following may be noticed: The
Flaming Terrapin *(1924),* Adamastor *(1928),* The Georgiad
(1931), Flowering Reeds *(1933),* Mithraic Emblems *(1936),*
Talking Bronco *(1940).* Broken Record *(1934) is a book of
reminiscences.*

'Poets in Africa' and 'The Palm' are both to be found in Sons of
the Mistral *(1941), a good selection of Campbell's poems. 'Poets in
Africa' is an early poem of which the author says, 'I very much
regret the mood of self-pity in which it was written,' but I include it
as an example of his attractive (if sometimes absurd), aggressive
verbal extravagance. 'The Palm', a later piece, moves nicely on its
tirsyllabic feet.*

Roy Campbell has suffered in appreciation for his championship of Franco during the Spanish Civil War. I think it relevant therefore to cite Wyndham Lewis's comment on Campbell's views:

Of politics he has none, unless they are such as go with a great antipathy for the English 'gentleman' in all his clubmanesque varieties; a great attachment to the back-Veldt of his native South Africa; and a constant desire to identify himself with the roughest and simplest of his fellow-creatures in pub., farm and bull-ring.

Poets in Africa

For grazing innocence a salad
Of lilies in the bud,
For those who dine on words a ballad,
For you and me a name of mud,
A rash of stars upon the sky,
A pox of flowers on the earth –
To such diseases of the eye
Habituated from our birth,

We had no time for make-believe
So early each began
To wear his liver on his sleeve,
To snarl, and be an angry man:
Far in the desert we have been
Where Nature, still to poets kind,
Admits no vegetable green
To soften the determined mind,

But with snarled gold and rumbled blue
Must disinfect the sight
Where once the tender maggots grew
Of faith and beauty and delight.
Each with a blister on his tongue,

Each with a crater in his tooth,
Our nerves are fire: we have been stung
By the tarantulas of truth.

Each like a freezing salamander
Impervious and immune,
No snivelling sentiment shall pander
To our flirtations with the moon,
And though with gay batrachian chirrup
Her poets thrill the swampy reach,
Not with so glutinous a syrup
As moonlight shall we grease our speech.

Our cook, the Sun, in craggy kitchens
Amid the howling waste
Has fried the terrible sour lichens
So dainty to a poet's taste,
Which sovereign remedy is ours
Against the earth's infectious scars,
Its annual eczema of flowers
The pullulation of its stars –

Whose itch corrodes the soft medulla
Of kindlier brains than ours
Wherein, attuned to local colour,
Each cheap colonial virtue flowers,
Flits like a moth from bloom to blossom
Or to protective markings trusts,
In shady corners playing possum
To gratify its private lusts.

The fauna of this mental waste,
They cheer our lonely way
And round our doleful footsteps haste
To skip, to gambol, and to play;
The kite of Mercy sails above

With reeking claws and cry that clangs,
The old grey wolf of Brother-Love
Slinks in our track with yellow fangs.

True sons of Africa are we,
Though bastardized with culture,
Indigenous, and wild, and free
As wolf, as pioneer and vulture –
Yea, though for us the vision blearing
No membrane nictitates the light,
Though we are cursed with sense and hearing
And doubly cursed with second sight,

Still doomed that skyward screech to hear
That haunted us in youth,
We shall grow terrible through fear,
We shall grow venomous with truth,
And through these plains where thought meanders
Through sheepish brains in wormy life,
Our lives shall roll like fierce Scamanders
Their red alluvium of strife.

When in the moonlight, red and bloody,
The night has smeared the plain,
We rise from awful nights of study
With coal-red eyes and whirling brain –
Our minds like dark destructive engines
Prepare those catapults and slings
In whose preliminary vengeance
The thunder of the Future sings.

What though we have no walls or bastions
To shield our riddled hearts? –
Arrowed like convicts, twin Sebastians
Each in his uniform of darts,
When in his crimson garb outlandish

The martyr turns a porcupine
Who such fearful spikes can brandish,
Who in more fiendish war-paint shine?

The Palm

Blistered and dry was the desert I trod
When out of the sky with the step of a god,
Victory-vanned, with her feathers out-fanned,
The palm tree alighting my journey delayed
And spread me, inviting, her carpet of shade.
Vain were evasions, though urgent my quest,
And there as the guest of her lovely persuasions
To lie in the shade of her branches was best.
Like a fountain she played, spilling plume over plume in
A golden cascade for the winds to illumine,
Ascending in brilliance and falling in shade,
And spurning the ground with a tiptoe resilience,
Danced to the sound of the music she made.
Her voice intervened on my shadowed seclusion
Like the whispered intrusion of seraph or fiend,
In its tone was the hiss of the serpent's wise tongue
But soft as the kiss of a lover it stung —
'Unstrung is your lute? For despair are you silent?
Am I not an island in oceans as mute?
Around me the thorns of the desert take root;
Though I spring from the rock of a region accurst,
Yet fair is the daughter of hunger and thirst
Who sings like the water the valleys have nursed,
And rings her blue shadow as deep and as cool
As the heavens of azure that sleep on a pool.
And you, who so soon by the toil were undone,
Could you guess through what horrors my beauty had won
Ere I crested the noon as the bride of the sun?
The roots are my anchor struck fast in the hill,
The higher I hanker, the deeper they drill,

Through the red mortar their claws interlock
To ferret the water through warrens of rock.
Each inch of my glory was wrenched with a groan,
Corroded with fire from the base of my throne
And drawn like a wire from the heart of a stone:
Though I soar in the height with a shape of delight
Uplifting my stem like the string of a kite,
Yet still must each grade of my climbing be told,
And still from the summit my measure I hold,
Sounding the azure with plummet of gold,
Partaking the strain of the heavenward pride
That soars me away from the earth I deride,
Though my stem be a rein that would tether me down
And fasten a chain on the height of my crown,
Yet through its tense nerve do I measure my might,
The strain of its curb is the strength of my flight:
And when, by the hate of the hurricane blown,
It doubles its forces with fibres that groan,
Exulting I ride in the tower of my pride
To feel that the strength of the blast is my own ...
Rest under my branches, breathe deep of my balm
From the hushed avalanches of fragrance and calm,
For suave is the silence that poises the palm.
The wings of the egrets are silken and fine,
But hushed with the secrets of Eden are mine:
Your spirit that grieves like the wind in my leaves
Shall be robbed of its care by those whispering thieves
To study my patience and hear, the day long,
The soft foliations of sand into song —
For bitter and cold though it rasp to my root,
Each atom of gold is the chance of a fruit,
The sap is the music, the stem is the flute,
And the leaves are the wings of the seraph I shape
Who dances, who springs in a golden escape,
Out of the dust and the drought of the plain,
To sing with the silver hosannas of rain.'

MICHAEL ROBERTS

Michael Roberts was born at Bournemouth in 1902 and educated at King's College, London and Trinity College, Cambridge. He was a schoolmaster in Newcastle-upon-Tyne (except for a break of three years in London) until he joined the B.B.C. European Service as General Intelligence Officer in 1941. His job was the collection of information from enemy-occupied countries. In 1943 he became editor of broadcasts for the clandestine press and contributed articles to underground papers in Belgium, France, Norway, etc. In 1945 he was appointed Principal of the College of St Mark and St John, Chelsea. He died in December, 1948.

Michael Roberts was an active propagandist for the new poetry of the 'thirties. His anthologies New Signatures *(1932) and* New Country *(1933) introduced and explained that poetry when it still seemed queer and difficult, and his* Critique of Poetry *(1934) and* Faber Book of Modern Verse, *which has a long, interesting introduction, attempted respectively to find an aesthetic for the movement and to set it in a perspective of the best modern verse (not forgetting, of course, Hopkins). Roberts also published three books of verse, a study of T. E. Hulme, a monograph on scientific method entitled* Newton and the Origin of Colours, *and other volumes of criticism.*

'The Castle' is reprinted from Orion Marches *(1939). There is an interpretation of the poem by Michael Roberts in Gwendolen Murphy's anthology,* The Modern Poet *(1938).*

The Castle

Words fall, words fail, like rocks, like falling stones;
Out of the towered clouds and the dark air,
Words fail, and a tree of blackness falls:
There is nothing at all to surrender or defend.

It was a grim castle, built in the bad years,
Built by an old man after years of failure,
Stuccoed with long complacency, and now
No more than an empty wineskin or a crushed fruit.

From the dark earth, the tree broke out, and men
Died with a frantic zeal, and spitting death:
Who knows what it was they died for?
Their bones are a fine dust, and their names forgotten.

Suburbs creep up the hill, and the trams are running,
Children find ghostly playmates in the ruins;
The sun glares on the emptiness, and vanished walls
Burn with a bitter death and unfulfilled perfection.

Stamp out the memory of old wars and lost causes:
Build a grave citadel of peace, or a tower of death:
The castle stands, inhuman, incorruptible,
Like a film before the eyes, or a mad vision.

WILLIAM PLOMER

*William Plomer was born at Pietersburg, N. Transvaal, in 1903
and educated at Rugby School. He has been a farmer in the Storm-
berg and a trader in Zululand, and has also travelled widely, having
lived at various times in Greece and Japan. Between 1940 and 1945
he served at the Admiralty. A long list of books, including novels,
short stories, biography and poetry, stands to his credit, and he has
edited* Kilvert's Diary *(1938–40) and the* Selected Poems of
Herman Melville *(1943).* Double Lives *(1943) is an autobiography of great subtlety and interest.*

Plomer's poetic output consists of several volumes – the earliest,
Notes for Poems, *is dated 1928 – but the reader may be referred to*

E 2

his Selected Poems *(1940) for a taste of the quality of his 'serious' verse. 'Father and Son: 1939' and 'A Ticket for the Reading Room' are from* The Dorking Thigh *(1945), a collection of satires. In a Prefatory Note to this book Mr Plomer writes:*

> *These satires are concerned with points in human experience at which the terrifying coincides with the absurd, the monstrous with the commonplace. Such points are perhaps commoner in our time than usual, for we have seen horror and absurdity on an enormous scale ... The satires are intended to be read aloud,* con brio.

They should also be read with Auden's ballads in mind and some of the early Betjeman pieces such as 'The Arrest of Oscar Wilde at the Cadogan Hotel.' William Plomer is less in love with his victims than John Betjeman, and he is less the moral psychologist than is the Auden of 'James Honeyman' and 'Miss Gee', but his effects are more pointed. 'A Ticket for the Reading Room' ends rather weakly, but such a counterpart to the seedy world of Graham Greene's novels was not to be resisted.

Father and Son: 1939

A family portrait not too stale to record
Of a pleasant old buffer, nephew to a lord,
Who believed that the bank was mightier than the sword,
And that an umbrella might pacify barbarians abroad
      Just like an old liberal
      Between the wars.

With an easy existence, and a cosy country place,
And with hardly a wrinkle, at sixty, in his face,
Growing old with old books, with old wine, and with grace,
Unaware that events move at a breakneck pace:
      Just like an old diehard
      Between the wars.

With innocuous tastes in common with his mate,
A love of his garden and his tidy snug estate,
Of dogs, music and children, and lying in bed late,
And no disposition to quarrel with his fate:
> Just like an old Englishman
> Between the wars.

With no religion or imagination, and a hazy lazy view
Of the great world where trouble kept cropping up anew,
With old clubmen for friends, who would seem stuffy to you,
Old faded prigs, but gentlemen (give them their due):
> Just like an old fossil
> Between the wars.

With a kindly old wife who subscribed for the oppressed,
With an O.B.E., and a coiffure like a last year's bird's nest,
Even more tolerant than anyone would have guessed,
Who hoped that in the long run all was for the best:
> Just like an old lady
> Between the wars.

With one child, a son, who in spite of his education
Showed only a modicum of common sense or cultivation,
Sometimes read the *Daily Worker* or the *New Statesman and
    Nation*.
But neither, it must be admitted, with much concentration:
> Just like a young fribble
> Between the wars.

With a firm grasp of half-truths, with political short-sight,
With a belief we could disarm but at the same time fight,
And that only the Left Wing could ever be right,
And that Moscow, of all places, was the sole source of light
> Just like a young hopeful
> Between the wars.

With a flash flat in Chelsea of a bogus elegance,
With surrealist pictures and books puffed by Gollancz,
With a degree of complacence which nothing could enhance,
And without one sole well-wisher to kick him in the pants:
        Just like a young smarty
        Between the wars.

With a precious mistress who thought she could paint
But could neither show respect nor exercise restraint,
Was a perfect goose-cap, and thought good manners quaint,
With affectation enough to try the patience of a saint:
        Just like a young cutie
        Between the wars.

With a succession of parties for sponges and bores,
With a traffic-jam outside (for they turned up in scores),
With first-rate sherry flowing into second-rate whores,
And third-rate conversation without one single pause:
        Just like a young couple
        Between the wars.

With week-ends in the country and holidays in France,
With promiscuous habits, time to sunbathe and dance,
And even to write books that were hardly worth a glance,
Earning neither reputation nor the publisher's advance:
        Just like a young writer
        Between the wars.

On a Sunday in September there were deck-chairs in the sun,
There was argument at lunch between the father and the son
(Smoke rose from Warsaw) for the beef was underdone
(Nothing points to heaven now but the anti-aircraft gun):
        With a hey nonny nonny
        And a hi-de-ho.

Oh, the 'twenties and the 'thirties were not otherwise designed
Than other times when blind men into ditches led the blind,

When the rich mouse ate the cheese and the poor mouse got the
    rind,
And man, the self-destroyer, was not lucid in his mind:
        With a hey nonny nonny
        And a hi-de-ho.

A Ticket for the Reading Room

        With a smile of secret triumph
          Seedy old untidy scholar,
        Inkstains on his finger-nails,
          Cobwebs on his Gladstone collar,

        Down at heel and out at elbows
          Off he goes on gouty feet
        (Where he goes his foxy smell goes),
          Off towards Great Russell Street.

        Unaware of other people,
          Peace and war and politics,
        Down the pavement see him totter
          Following his *idée fixe*.

        Past the rowdy corner café
          Full of Cypriots and flies
        Where the customers see daggers
          Looking from each other's eyes,

        Past the sad but so-called Fun Fair
          Where a few immortal souls
        Occupy their leisure hours
          Shooting little balls at holes,

        Past the window full of booklets,
          Rubber goods and cures for piles,
         Past the pub, the natty milk-bar
          Crowded with galactophiles,

Through the traffic, down the side-street
    Where an unfrocked parson thrives
('Palmist and Psychologist')
    Cutting short unwanted lives,

Through the shady residential
    Square in which a widow runs
A quiet gambling-hell, or 'bridge club',
    Fleecing other women's sons,

On he shuffles, quietly mumbling
    Figures, facts and formulæ –
Bats are busy in the belfry,
    In the bonnet hums a bee.

At the Reading Room he settles
    Pince-nez on his bottle nose,
Reads and scribbles, reads and scribbles,
    Till the day draws to a close,

Then returns to oh, what squalor!
    Kippers, cake and dark brown tea,
Filthy sheets and filthier blankets,
    Sleep disturbed by mouse and flea.

What has the old man been doing?
    What's his game? Another book?
He is out to pour contempt on
    Esperanto, Vōlapük,

To fake a universal language
    Full of deft abbreviation
For the day when all mankind
    Join and form one happy nation.

In this the poor old chap resembles
    Prosperous idealists
Who talk as if men reached for concord
    With their clenched or grasping fists.

CECIL DAY LEWIS

Cecil Day Lewis, who with Auden and Spender formed the original political-cum-poetical triumvirate of the 'thirties, was born in Ireland in 1904 and educated at Sherborne School and Wadham College, Oxford. He edited Oxford Poetry *with W. H. Auden in 1927, and, after leaving the University, became a schoolmaster in turn at Oxford, Helensburgh and Cheltenham until 1935. He was employed at the Ministry of Information during the war. Since then he has been occupied with writing, lecturing and broadcasting.*

He is primarily a poet, but he has written novels – The Friendly Tree *(1936),* Starting Point *(1937) and* Child of Misfortune *(1939) may be mentioned – as well as detective fiction (under a pseudonym) and stories for children, of which the most recent example is* The Otterbury Incident *(1948). His criticism includes* A Hope for Poetry *(1934),* Poetry for You *(1945) – a book much used now in schools – and* The Poetic Image *(1947), which is the published form of his Clark Lectures at Cambridge in 1946.*

Mr Day Lewis has a large published output in verse. Collected Poems 1929–1936 *(1948) contains his work up to that time including both the pre-political poetry of* From Feathers to Iron, *perhaps his best collection until* Word Over All *(1943), and the rather strident tub-thumping and pylon-praising of* The Magnetic Mountain. *Later books include* Overtures to Death *(1938), the excellent translations of* The Georgics of Virgil *(1940),* Word Over All *(1943) and* Poems 1943–1947 *(1948), a volume of personal lyrics in which the influence of Thomas Hardy and Edward Thomas is very marked.*

Stephen Spender has observed that Day Lewis is a poet 'who is least sure of himself when he writes of his immediate feelings'. This statement can be accepted if certain lyrics, such as 'Marriage of Two' and 'The Woman Alone', from Day Lewis's latest collection, can be taken as exceptions proving the rule. As a personal lyric poet, it is true, he sometimes fumbles and produces blurred or trite effects. His abilities as a translator or as a narrative poet – a good specimen is 'The Nabara' from Overtures to Death *– can rarely be questioned in this way.* Poems 1943–1947 *contains an excellent example of translation in 'The Graveyard by the Sea', a version of Paul Valéry's 'Cimetière Marin'.*

The four poems given here are arranged in chronological order. 'You that love England', the first and weakest, is the only one from the strongly political phase. In brief it may be said that Day Lewis's failures are verbal, his successes rhythmical. This is, of course, a simplification, but the greater pleasure to be derived from his later volumes is more due, I think, to an increased power of making rhythmical patterns than to any change in subject-matter or attitude.

You That Love England

You that love England, who have an ear for her music,
The slow movement of clouds in benediction,
Clear arias of light thrilling over her uplands,
Over the chords of summer sustained peacefully;
Ceaseless the leaves' counterpoint in a west wind lively,
Blossom and river rippling loveliest allegro,
And the storms of wood strings brass at year's finale:
Listen. Can you not hear the entrance of a new theme?

You who go out alone, on tandem or on pillion,
Down arterial roads riding in April,
Or sad beside lakes where hill-slopes are reflected
Making fires of leaves, your high hopes fallen:
Cyclists and hikers in company, day excursionists,
Refugees from cursed towns and devastated areas;
Know you seek a new world, a saviour to establish
Long-lost kinship and restore the blood's fulfilment.

You who like peace, good sticks, happy in a small way
Watching birds or playing cricket with schoolboys,
Who pay for drinks all round, whom disaster chose not;
Yet passing derelict mills and barns roof-rent
Where despair has burnt itself out — hearts at a standstill,
Who suffer loss, aware of lowered vitality;
We can tell you a secret, offer a tonic; only
Submit to the visiting angel, the strange new healer.

You above all who have come to the far end, victims
Of a run-down machine, who can bear it no longer;
Whether in easy chairs chafing at impotence
Or against hunger, bullies and spies preserving
The nerve for action, the spark of indignation —
Need fight in the dark no more, you know your enemies.
You shall be leaders when zero hour is signalled,
Wielders of power and welders of a new world.

Passage from Childhood

His earliest memory, the mood
Fingered and frail as maidenhair,
Was this — a china cup somewhere
In a green, deep wood.
He lives to find again somewhere
That wood, that homely cup; to taste all
Its chill, imagined dews; to dare
The dangerous crystal.

Who can say what misfeatured elf
First led him into that lifelong
Passage of mirrors where, so young,
He saw himself
Balanced as Blondin, more headstrong
Than baby Hercules, rare as a one-
Cent British Guiana, above the wrong
And common run?

He knew the secrecy of squirrels,
The foolish doves' antiphony,
And what wrens fear. He was gun-shy,
Hating all quarrels.
Life was a hostile land to spy,
Full of questions he dared not ask
Lest the answer in mockery
Or worse unmask.

Quick to injustice, quick he grew
This hermit and contorted shell.
Self-pity like a thin rain fell,
Fouling the view:
Then tree-trunks seemed wet roots of hell,
Wren or catkin might turn vicious,
The dandelion clock could tell
Nothing auspicious.

No exile has ever looked so glum
With the pines fretful overhead,
Yet he felt at home in the gothic glade –
More than at home.
You will forgive him that he played
Bumble-puppy on the small mossed lawn
All by himself for hours, afraid
Of being born.

Lying awake one night, he saw
Eternity stretched like a howl of pain:
He was tiny and terrible, a new pin
On a glacier's floor.
Very few they are who have lain
With eternity and lived to tell it:
There's a secret process in his brain
And he cannot sell it.

Now, beyond reach of sense or reason,
His life walks in a glacial sleep
For ever, since he drank that cup
And found it poison.
He's one more ghost, engaged to keep
Eternity's long hours and mewed
Up in live flesh with no escape
From solitude.

The Poet

For me there is no dismay
Though ills enough impend.
I have learned to count each day
Minute by breathing minute —
Birds that lightly begin it,
Shadows muting its end —
As lovers count for luck
Their own heart-beats and believe
In the forest of time they pluck
Eternity's single leaf.

Tonight the moon's at the full.
Full moon's the time for murder.
But I look to the clouds that hide her —
The bay below me is dull,
An unreflecting glass —
And chafe for the clouds to pass,
And wish she suddenly might
Blaze down at me so I shiver
Into a twelve-branched river
Of visionary light.

For now imagination,
My royal, impulsive swan,
With raking flight – I can see her –
Comes down as it were upon
A lake in whirled snow-floss
And flurry of spray like a skier
Checking. Again I feel
The wounded waters heal.
Never before did she cross
My heart with such exaltation.

Oh, on this striding edge,
This hare-bell height of calm
Where intuitions swarm
Like nesting gulls and knowledge
Is free as the winds that blow,
A little while sustain me,
Love, till my answer is heard!
Oblivion roars below,
Death's cordon narrows: but vainly,
If I've slipped the carrier word.

Dying, any man may
Feel wisdom harmonious, fateful
At the tip of his dry tongue.
All I have felt or sung
Seems now but the moon's fitful
Sleep on a clouded bay,
Swan's maiden flight, or the climb
To a tremulous, hare-bell crest.
Love, tear the song from my breast!
Short, short is the time.

The Unwanted

On a day when the breath of roses
    Plumpened a swooning breeze
And all the silken combes of summer
    Opened wide their knees,
Between two sighs they planted one —
A willed one, a wanted one —
And he will be the sign, they said, of our felicities.

Eager the loins he sprang from,
    Happy the sheltering heart:
Seldom had the seed of man
    So charmed, so clear a start.
And he was born as frail a one,
As ailing, freakish, pale a one
As ever the wry planets knotted their beams to thwart.

Sun locked up for winter;
    Earth an empty rind:
Two strangers harshly flung together
    As by a flail of wind.
Oh was it not a furtive thing,
A loveless, damned, abortive thing —
This flurry of the groaning dust, and what it left behind!

Sure, from such warped beginnings
    Nothing debonair
Can come? But neither shame nor panic,
    Drugs nor sharp despair
Could uproot that untoward thing,
That all too fierce and froward thing:
Willy-nilly born it was, divinely formed and fair.

PETER QUENNELL

Peter Quennell was born in 1905, his mother being the historian Marjorie Quennell, and educated at Berkhamsted and Balliol College, Oxford. He became a contributor to various reviews and periodicals such as The New Statesman, Life and Letters *and* The Criterion, *and in 1930 he accepted the Chair of English Literature in the Government University at Tokyo. He visited the United States in 1938 and is now editor of* The Cornhill Magazine.

Mr Quennell has published a novel, The Phoenix Kind (1931), *and a collection of short stories,* Sympathy and Other Stories (1933). *He is also the author of a study,* Baudelaire and the Symbolists (1929), *and the editor of an anthology of Metaphysical poetry,* Aspects of Seventeenth Century Verse (1933). *These books are probably less known to the general public than his biographical studies of Byron (on whom he is an authority). His most recent book,* Ruskin (1949), *is also a biography.*

'The Flight into Egypt' is from Poems (1926), *a collection unduly neglected – probably because Mr Quennell has published no later poems. His writings, both in prose and verse, have a characteristic elegance, and the poem given here seems to me a very favourable example of the free verse of the 'twenties. It is earlier than Eliot's* Journey of the Magi (1927), *by which at one time I imagined it to be superficially influenced.*

The Flight into Egypt

Within Heaven's circle I had not guessed at this,
I had not guessed at pleasure such as this,
So sharp a pleasure,
That, like a lamp burning in foggy night,
Makes its own orb and sphere of flowing gold
And tents itself in light.

Going before you, now how many days,
Thoughts, all turned back like birds against the wind,
Wheeled sullenly towards my Father's house,
Considered his blind presence and the gathered, bustling pæan,
The affluence of his sweetness, his grace and unageing might.

My flesh glowed then in the shadow of a loose cloak
And my brightness troubled the ground with every pulse of the
     blood,
My wings lax on the air, my eyes open and grave,
With the vacant pride of hardly less than a god.

We passed thickets that quaked with hidden deer,
And wide shallows dividing before my feet,
Empty plains threaded, and between stiff aloes
I took the ass's bridle to climb into mountain pathways.

When cold bit you, through your peasant's mantle,
And my Father filled the air with meaningless stars,
I brought dung and dead white grass for fuel,
Blowing a fire with the breath of the holy word.

Your drudge, Joseph, slept; you would sit unmoving,
In marble quiet, or by the unbroken voice of a river,
Would sometimes bare your maiden breast to his mouth,
The suckling, to the conscious God balanced upon your knees.

Apart I considered the melodious names of my brothers,
As again in my Father's house, and the even spheres
Slowly, nightlong recalled the splendour of numbers;
I heard again the voluptuous measure of praise.

Sometimes pacing beneath clarity immeasurable
I saw my mind lie open and desert,
The wavering streams frozen up and each coppice quieted,
A whole valley in starlight with leaves and waters.

Coming at last to these farthest Syrian hills,
Attis or Adon, some ambushed lust looked out;
My skin grows pale and smooth, shrunken as silk,
Without the rough effulgence of a God.

And here no voice has spoken;
There is no shrine of any godhead here
No grove or hallowed fires,
And godhead seems asleep.

Only the vine has woven
Strange houses and blind rooms and palaces,
Into each hollow and crevice continually
Dropped yearlong irrecoverable flowers.

The sprawling vine has built us a close room,
Obedient Hymen fills the air with mist;
And to make dumb our theft
The white and moving sand that will not bear a print.

REX WARNER

Rex Warner was born in 1905 and his boyhood was spent in Gloucestershire, where his father was a clergyman of the Church of England. He was educated at St George's, Harpenden, and Wadham College, Oxford, where he studied Classics and English. Since then he has taught these subjects in schools in England and Egypt. During the war he was a schoolmaster in the London area, and for some time after it he was in Athens as Director of the British Council there. His Poems *were first published in 1937. They were re-issued in a revised edition as* Poems and Contradictions *(1945). He has also published four novels:* The Wild Goose Chase *(1936),* The Professor *(1938),* The Aerodrome *(1941) and* Why Was I Killed? *(1943); a book of essays,* The Cult of Power *(1946); and two translations, Euripides'* Medea *(1944) and the* Prometheus Bound *of Aeschylus (1947).*

Rex Warner was friendly with Auden and Day Lewis at Oxford, and this association is commemorated by a banal couplet in The Magnetic Mountain:

> *Then I'll hit the trail for that promising land;*
> *May catch up with Wystan and Rex my friend ...*

and by the fourth ode of 'Six Odes' in Auden's The Orators. *But he is to be thought of as a novelist rather than as a poet. There is a symposium on his novels and their relation to Kafka's work in* Focus One (1945), *edited by B. Rajan and A. Pearse.*

Nile Fishermen

Naked men, fishing in Nile without a licence,
kneedeep in it, pulling gaunt at stretched ropes.
Round the next bend is the police boat and the officials
ready to make an arrest on the yellow sand.

The splendid bodies are stark to the swimming sand,
taut to the ruffled water, the flickering palms,
yet swelling and quivering as they tug at the trembling ropes.
Their faces are bent along the arms and still.

Sun is torn in coloured petals on the water,
the water shivering in the heat and the north wind;
and near and far billow out white swollen crescents,
the clipping wings of feluccas, seagull sails.

A plunge in the turbid water, a quick joke stirs
a flashing of teeth, an invocation of God.
Here is food to be fetched and living from labour.
The tight ropes strain and the glittering backs for the haul.

Round the bend comes the police boat. The men scatter.
The officials blow their whistles on the golden sand.
They overtake and arrest strong bodies of men
who follow with sullen faces, and leave their nets behind.

NORMAN CAMERON

Norman Cameron was born in India in 1905 and educated at Fettes College and Oriel College, Oxford. After leaving the university he was for a while a superintendent of education in Southern Nigeria before becoming an advertising copy-writer in London. In the 'thirties he contributed frequently to Geoffrey Grigson's New Verse *and to* Epilogue, *the miscellany issued by Robert Graves and Laura Riding. He was awarded the M.B.E. for work on propaganda to German troops in Italy during the war, and he was with the British Forces in Austria until early in 1947, when he returned to his work in advertising.*

He has brought out the following books of verse: The Winter House *(1935) and, with Robert Graves and Alan Hodge,* Work in Hand *(1942). He has also published* Select Verse Poems of Arthur Rimbaud *(1942), a volume of translations. 'Naked Among the Trees' and 'The Invader' are from his first and second books of verse respectively. Edwin Muir has described him as 'a neat, semi-epigrammatic poet', but this is a tepid way of referring to his precision and skill with words.* The Winter House *is a collection in which no single poem appears to have been forced.*

Naked Among the Trees

Formerly he had been a well-loved god,
Each visit from him a sweet episode,
Not like the outrageous Pentecostal rush
Or wilful Jahveh shrieking from a bush.

He bloomed in our bodies to the finger-tips
And rose like barley-sugar round the lips,
Then unawares was cleanly gone away,
With no relapse or aftertaint to pay.

We've forced the burgeoned lust he gave to us
Into a thousand manners of misuse,
Into the hot alarms, wishes and frets,
The drinking-bouts, the boasting and the bets.

And these have made his cult degenerate,
So that the booted Puritan magistrate
Did right to spur down on the devotees,
Catch them and whip them naked among the trees.

The Invader

Our shops and farms wide open lie;
Still the invader feels a lack:
Disquiet whets his gluttony
For what he may not carry back.

He prowls about in search of wealth
But has no skill to recognize
Our things of worth: we need no stealth
To mask them from his pauper eyes.

He calls for worship and amaze;
We give him yes-men in a row,
Reverberating that self-praise
He wearied of a while ago.

He casts around for some new whim,
Something preposterously more:
'Love me' he bids. We offer him
The slack embraces of a whore.

And when he spitefully makes shift
To share with us his pauperdom,
By forcing on us as a gift
The shoddy wares he brought from home,

And watches that we sell and buy
Amongst us his degrading trash,
He gets no gain at all. Though sly
With what he knows, the guns and cash,

What he knows not he may not touch:
Those very spoils for which he came
Are still elusive to his clutch –
They swerve and scorch him like a flame.

Invader-outcast of all lands,
He lives condemned to gorge and crave,
To foul his feast with his own hands:
At once the oppressor and the slave.

VERNON WATKINS

*Vernon Watkins was born in Wales in 1906 and educated at
Repton and Magdalene College, Cambridge. He now works in a
bank in Swansea. He wrote verse for many years without printing
it and issued his first volume,* The Ballad of the Mari Lwyd, *only
in 1941, when he was thirty-five years old.* The Lamp and the Veil,
*which consists of three long poems, appeared in 1945, and his latest
collection,* The Lady with the Unicorn, *containing shorter pieces
written since 1941, was published in 1948 – too late, I may interpolate, to be of use in compiling this anthology. Vernon Watkins is
a poet, it is said, who prefers to revise or discard poems rather than
print them, and his publishers remark on the difficulty they had in
inducing him to bring out* The Lady with the Unicorn.

*The passage by which Watkins is represented here is the ninth
section of 'The Broken Sea' from* The Lamp and the Veil.
*Although I have read the two earlier volumes of verse several times,
I do not feel able to make a concise judgment on Vernon Watkins as*

a poet with any confidence. He is certainly one of the most accom-
plished writers of verse to have emerged since 1939, and, if his
movement is sometimes so loose that a weakness of structure
becomes apparent in the longer pieces, he is generally able to sustain
his musical idiom satisfyingly in a way that is unusual to-day.

From *The Broken Sea*

My lamp that was lit every night has burnt a hole in the shade.
A seawave plunges. Listen. Below me crashes the bay.
The rushing greedy water smothers the talk of the spade.
Now, on the sixth of November, I remember the tenth of May.

I was going to fly to your christening to give you a cup.
Here, like Andersen's tailor, I weave the invisible thread.
The burnt-out clock of St Mary's has come to a stop,
And the hand still points to the figure that beckons the house-
stoned dead.

Child Shades of my ignorant darkness, I mourn that moment
alive
Near the glow-lamped Eumenides' house, overlooking the ships
in flight,
Where Pearl White focussed our childhood, near the foot of
Cwmdonkin Drive,
To a figment of crime stampeding in the posters' wind-blown
blight.

I regret the broken Past, its prompt and punctilious cares,
All the villainies of the fire-and-brimstone-visited town.
I miss the painter of limbo at the top of the fragrant stairs,
The extravagant hero of night, his iconoclastic frown.

Through the criminal thumb-prints of soot, in the swaddling-
　　bands of a shroud,
I pace the familiar street, and the wall repeats my pace,
Alone in the blown-up city, lost in a bird-voiced crowd
Murdered where shattering breakers at your pillow's head leave
　　lace.

For death has burst upon you, yet your light-flooded eyes do
　　not tremble
Where pictures for waking life stand in the spray's wild bead.
You are guarded, shrined in the torrent, fast-locked in the cave
　　of the Sibyl,
In that terrifying delay of the waters' magical speed.

Asleep to-night in Paris, not knowing I walk your world,
You are deaf to the schoolyard's voices, where, escaped, the
　　children meet,
The world of a child's one town, renascent, in rage unfurled
Between Cwmdonkin railing and black-faced Inkerman Street.

Waves, hooded, raging, thunder, hiding contagious guilt,
Tossing, high on the shale, the hard and scribbled stones.
An anchor's dirge is buried under the waters' quilt.
Dazzling sunbeams have hidden the hook and the barnacled
　　bones.

O indifferent grains of sand, O mother-of-pearl of the shell,
I hear the inconstant water, the blind, the wandering one.
The groan of Sophocles, and the groan of the leper's bell
Burst on annihilation: through your window breaks the sun.

I hear the breath of the storm. The engulfed, Gargantuan tide,
Heaped in hills by the moles, hurls to the mountain's head
The streets of sunrise. O windows burning on Townhill side,
O light of annunciation, unearthing the unknown dead!

JOHN BETJEMAN

John Betjeman — poet, topographer and churchwarden — was born in 1906 and educated at Marlborough and at Oxford, where he was a contemporary of Auden and MacNeice. He has been for some time a book critic for the Daily Herald. *He is the author of various Shell Guides and editor (with John Piper, the painter) of the first volume in John Murray's new illustrated County Guides Series,* Murray's Buckinghamshire Guide *(1948). He has also written the following works in prose :* Ghastly Good Taste *(1933),* An Oxford University Chest *(1938), and* Antiquarian Prejudice *(1939).*

Mr Betjeman has published several books of verse. Continual Dew *(1937),* Old Lights for New Chancels *(1940) and* New Bats in Old Belfries *(1944) may be mentioned, together with* Selected Poems *(1948) chosen and introduced by John Sparrow. This last collection contains new poems and revised versions of old favourites.*

John Betjeman writes the nature poetry of the devastated Home Counties and is the laureate of material ordinarily considered anti-poetic — 'I love suburbs and gas-lights and Pont Street and Gothic Revival churches and mineral railways, provincial towns and garden cities.' This is the ordinary view of his work; it is at least half-true, and the poet has been glad enough to shelter behind it. Of this vein John Summerson has written appreciatively: 'Why are memories of gas-lit Congregational Chapels so moving? Why is there music in the preamble of Kelly's Directory? Why is the ugly and the second-rate so often charged with poetry when it gets old, worn an forgotten? Answer these questions and you will know why Betjeman's poetry is poetry.' Half-true, it is agreed, but Selected Poems *also reveals a serious landscape artist in verse, who finds his landscapes far outside the Home Counties, and in 'Before the Anæsthetic' a writer of personal lyric — a poem, says Mr Sparrow, 'in which he comes near, or as near as he has yet allowed himself, to laying bare his most intimate feelings'.*

'Death in Leamington' is reprinted from Continual Dew. *It represents the earlier, more facetious Betjeman and is relegated by Mr Sparrow – who calls it, very happily, the poet's 'Innisfree' – to the juvenilia of* Selected Poems. *'The Planster's Vision' and 'May-Day Song for North Oxford' are from* New Bats in Old Belfries. *The first is satirical, even angry; the second is satirical-lyrical, as Polonius would have said. The satirical element has been pruned, if not excised, in the shorter version in* Selected Poems, *entitled 'Spring Morning in North Oxford'.*

The Planster's Vision

Cut down that timber! Bells, too many and strong,
    Pouring their music through the branches bare,
    From moon-white church-towers down the windy air
Have pealed the centuries out with Evensong.
Remove those cottages, a huddled throng!
    Too many babies have been born in there,
    Too many coffins, bumping down the stair,
Carried the old their garden paths along.

I have a Vision of The Future, chum,
    The workers' flats in fields of soya beans
      Tower up like silver pencils, score on score:
And Surging Millions hear the Challenge come
    From microphones in communal canteens
      'No Right! No Wrong! All's perfect, evermore.'

May-Day Song for North Oxford

(Annie Laurie Tune)

Bellbroughton Road is bonny, and pinkly bursts the spray
Of prunus and forsythia across the public way,
For a full spring-tide of blossom seethed and departed hence,
Leaving land-locked pools of jonquils by sunny garden fence.

And a constant sound of flushing runneth from windows where
The toothbrush too is airing in this new North Oxford air;
From Summerfields to Lynam's, the thirsty tarmac dries,
And a Cherwell mist dissolveth on elm-discovering skies.

Oh! well-bound Wells and Bridges! Oh! earnest ethical search
For the wide high-table λογος of St C. S. Lewis's Church.
This diamond-eyed Spring morning my soul soars up the slope
Of a right good rough-cast buttress on the housewall of my
    hope.

And open-necked and freckled, where once there grazed the
    cows,
Emancipated children swing on old apple boughs,
And pastel-shaded book rooms bring New Ideas to birth
As the whitening hawthorn only hears the heart beat of the
    earth.

Death in Leamington

She died in the upstairs bedroom
    By the light of the ev'ning star
That shone through the plate glass window
    From over Leamington Spa.

Beside her the lonely crochet
    Lay patiently and unstirred,
But the fingers that would have work'd it
    Were dead as the spoken word.

And Nurse came in with the tea-things
    Breast high 'mid the stands and chairs —
But Nurse was alone with her own little soul,
    And the things were alone with theirs.

She bolted the big round window,
     She let the blinds unroll,
She set a match to the mantle,
     She covered the fire with coal.

And 'Tea!' she said in a tiny voice
     'Wake up! It's nearly *five*.'
Oh! Chintzy, chintzy cheeriness,
     Half dead and half alive!

Do you know that the stucco is peeling?
     Do you know that the heart will stop?
From those yellow Italianate arches
     Do you hear the plaster drop?

Nurse looked at the silent bedstead,
     At the gray, decaying face,
As the calm of a Leamington ev'ning
     Drifted into the place.

She moved the table of bottles
     Away from the bed to the wall,
And tiptoeing gently over the stairs
     Turned down the gas in the hall.

WILLIAM EMPSON

William Empson was born in Yorkshire in 1906 and educated at Winchester and Magdalene College, Cambridge, where he distinguished himself in mathematics and literature. He has occupied Chairs of English Literature in China and Japan. As a critic he is known by two stimulating books: Seven Types of Ambiguity

(1930) and Some Versions of Pastoral *(1935). He has also published two collections of verse,* Poems *(1935) and* The Gathering Storm *(1940). Both of these contain notes, which are sometimes helpful in interpreting poems often extraordinarily difficult because of their intricacy of thought. Empson is a man of intellect, knowledgeable about the sciences, trained to be precise in language. In his poems he seems to be almost exclusively concerned with saying something to make it clear to himself (and incidentally to a few like-minded readers), and the problem of communication, which worried so many poets in the 'thirties, therefore remains a side-issue. The ideal reader of Empson would have to be a specialist like Empson, and, because of personal references and allusions in his books, also an intimate friend of the poet.*

The three poems given here are all taken from The Gathering Storm. *I have chosen poems I understand, or think I understand, and therefore can admire. What I admire is the pertinacity with which a subject is teased out and the unsentimental statement of the teasing. There are some poems I cannot understand at all.*

Aubade

Hours before dawn we were woken by the quake.
My house was on a cliff. The thing could take
Bookloads off shelves, break bottles in a row.
Then the long pause and then the bigger shake.
It seemed the best thing to be up and go.

And far too large for my feet to step by.
I hoped that various buildings were brought low.
The heart of standing is you cannot fly.

It seemed quite safe till she got up and dressed.
The guarded tourist makes the guide the test.
Then I said The Garden? Laughing she said No.
Taxi for her and for me healthy rest.
It seemed the best thing to be up and go.

The language problem but you have to try.
Some solid ground for lying could she show?
The heart of standing is you cannot fly.

None of these deaths were her point at all.
The thing was that being woken he would bawl
And finding her not in earshot he would know.
I tried saying Half an Hour to pay this call.
It seemed the best thing to be up and go.

I slept, and blank as that I would yet lie.
Till you have seen what a threat holds below,
The heart of standing is you cannot fly.

Tell me again about Europe and her pains,
Who's tortured by the drought, who by the rains.
Glut me with floods where only the swine can row
Who cuts his throat and let him count his gains.
It seemed the best thing to be up and go.

A bedshift flight to a Far Eastern sky.
Only the same war on a stronger toe.
The heart of standing is you cannot fly.

Tell me more quickly what I lost by this,
Or tell me with less drama what they miss
Who call no die a god for a good throw,
Who say after two aliens had one kiss
It seemed the best thing to be up and go.

But as to risings, I can tell you why.
It is on contradiction that they grow.
It seemed the best thing to be up and go.
Up was the heartening and the strong reply.
The heart of standing is we cannot fly.

Reflection from Rochester

'But wretched Man is still in arms for Fear.'

'From fear to fear, successively betrayed' —
By making risks to give a cause for fear
(Feeling safe with causes, and from birth afraid),

By climbing higher not to look down, by mere
Destruction of the accustomed because strange
(Too complex a loved system, or too clear),

By needing change but not too great a change
And therefore a new fear — man has achieved
All the advantage of a wider range,

Successfully has the first fear deceived,
Though the wheels run on sleepers. This is not
The law of nature it has been believed.

Increasing power (it has increased a lot)
Embarrasses 'attempted suicides',
Narrows their margin. Policies that got

'Virility from war' get much besides;
The mind, as well in mining as in gas
War's parallel, now less easily decides

On a good root-confusion to amass
Much safety from irrelevant despair.
Mere change in numbers made the process crass.

We now turn blank eyes for a pattern there
Where first the race of armament was made;
Where a less involute compulsion played.
'For hunger or for love they bite and tear.'

Courage Means Running

Fearful 'had the root of the matter', bringing
Him things to fear, and he read well that ran;
Muchafraid went over the river singing,

Though none knew what she sang. Usual for a man
Of Bunyan's courage to respect fear. It is the two
Most exquisite surfaces of knowledge can

Get clap (the other is the eye). Steadily you
Should clean your teeth, for your own weapon's near
Your own throat always. No purpose, view,

Or song but's weak if without the ballast of fear.
We fail to hang on those firm times that met
And knew a fear because when simply here

It does not suggest its transformation. Yet
To escape emotion (a common hope) and attain
Cold truth is essentially to get

Out by a rival emotion fear. We gain
Truth, to put it sanely, by gift of pleasure
And courage, but, since pleasure knits with pain,

Both presume fear. To take fear as the measure
May be a measure of self-respect. Indeed
As the operative clue in seeking treasure

Is normally trivial and the urgent creed
To balance enough possibles; as both bard
And hack must blur or peg lest you misread;

As to be hurt is petty, and to be hard
Stupidity; as the economists raise
Bafflement to a boast we all take as guard;

As the wise patience of England is a gaze
Over the drop, and 'high' policy means clinging;
There is not much else that we dare to praise.

LOUIS MACNEICE

Louis MacNeice was born at Belfast in 1907 of Irish parents – his father being Bishop of Down, Connor and Dromore – and educated at Marlborough and Merton College, Oxford. He took a first in Classical Mods. and Greats and was appointed a Lecturer in Classics at Birmingham University in 1930. He went to Bedford College, London, in 1936 as a Lecturer in Greek. In the same year he visited Spain and (with Auden) Iceland – the second journey in order to write Letters *from Iceland. He visited America early in 1939 to lecture at various universities, and he was Lecturer in Poetry at Cornell University in the first part of 1940. Since 1941 he has been a member of the staff of the B.B.C., engaged in writing and producing radio plays and features.*

In the thirties Louis MacNeice was a contributor to New Verse *and his name was closely linked with the names of Auden and Spender. But even then he was more shy of politics than either of his friends. 'If the writer is political at all,' he said, 'it is his special function to preserve his critical faculty. He must not see things (such as the Spanish War) purely in terms of black and white.' More can be discovered of his attitude to politics and of the course of his poetic development in his sound, unpretentious primer,* Modern Poetry *(1938).*

MacNeice published what he calls 'a book of juvenile poems' in 1929, but his first serious book of verse was Poems *(1935). Apart from travel-books and a study of Yeats, he has published the following since then: a verse-translation,* The Agamemnon of Aeschylus *(1936); a poetic drama,* Out of the Picture *(1937), strongly influenced by the Auden-Isherwood plays;* The Dark

Tower (*1947*), *a collection of plays for radio; and five volumes of verse. These five are* The Earth Compels (*1938*), Autumn Journal (*1939*), Plant and Phantom (*1941*), Springboard (*1944*), *and* Holes in the Sky (*1948*). *His* Collected Poems *appeared in 1949.*

I have represented MacNeice in this anthology by poems from all his books of verse except the verse-diary Autumn Journal *and* Holes in the Sky (*which came too recently to hand*). *As the poems will show, there is not much development to record, certainly none of the conversions and re-conversions to be noticed in the poetic careers, say, of Auden or Day Lewis. It is hard to trace even a technical development in his work. He was attempting the eclogue and the long ode in* Poems (*1935*), *and even 'The Kingdom' in* Springboard (*1944*) *is no more ambitious than these and in the opinion of some critics (including myself) less successful. Mac-Neice's virtues include a fine sense of colour, a satirical and observant eye, and a lively interest in words, rhymes and rhythms. All his collections contain good poems. The variety of this goodness is to be noted: he has written excellent love poetry, successful dramatic lyrics or character sketches like the 'Novelettes' of* Plant and Phantom (*from which I reprint 'Les Sylphides'*), *humorous and satirical verse like 'Bagpipe Music', argumentative and reflective poems like 'Plurality'. He can celebrate the ordinary and the everyday without putting his tongue in his cheek, because the imperviousness — except in time of war — of the ordinary man to politics, creeds and -isms strikes a sympathetic chord in MacNeice. He almost always writes well of Ireland. His best work was unequalled in the 'thirties for its gaiety, grace and a lightness which was never silly or ostrich-like.*

'The Kingdom' from Springboard *seems to hint at a more serious defence of the individual as the safest repository of human values. This poem should be compared with Auden's 'September 1, 1939' from* Another Time (*1940*), *and both poems should be placed alongside Mr E. M. Forster's essay in the symposium,* I Believe (*1940*). *This essay sketches a philosophy of personal relations and employs ideas and even phrases which are repeated in the pieces by Auden and MacNeice.*

The limitations of MacNeice's poetry, when it is thought of

*beside the best work of Auden and Spender, seem to be due to a
certain devil-may-care lack of seriousness. He is too eager and
impatient to accept his subject quietly and try to understand it. He
grabs it, pats it into various shapes, and varnishes any cracks in the
quality of his perception with his prestidigitatory skill with words
and images.*

Snow

The room was suddenly rich and the great bay-window was
Spawning snow and pink roses against it
Soundlessly collateral and incompatible:
World is suddener than we fancy it.

World is crazier and more of it than we think,
Incorrigibly plural. I peel and portion
A tangerine and spit the pips and feel
The drunkenness of things being various.

And the fire flames with a bubbling sound for world
Is more spiteful and gay than one supposes —
On the tongue on the eyes on the ears in the palms of one's
        hands —
There is more than glass between the snow and the huge roses.

Bagpipe Music

It's no go the merrygoround, it's no go the rickshaw,
All we want is a limousine and a ticket for the peepshow.
Their knickers are made of crêpe-de-chine, their shoes are made
        of python,
Their halls are lined with tiger rugs and their walls with heads of
        bison.

John MacDonald found a corpse, put it under the sofa,
Waited till it came to life and hit it with a poker,
Sold its eyes for souvenirs, sold its blood for whiskey,
Kept its bones for dumb-bells to use when he was fifty.

It's no go the Yogi-Man, it's no go Blavatsky,
All we want is a bank balance and a bit of skirt in a taxi.

Annie MacDougall went to milk, caught her foot in the heather,
Woke to hear a dance record playing of Old Vienna.
It's no go your maidenheads, it's no go your culture,
All we want is a Dunlop tyre and the devil mend the puncture.

The Laird o' Phelps spent Hogmanay declaring he was sober,
Counted his feet to prove the fact and found he had one foot
    over.
Mrs Carmichael had her fifth, looked at the job with repulsion,
Said to the midwife 'Take it away; I'm through with over-
    production'.

It's no go the gossip column, it's no go the Ceilidh,
All we want is a mother's help and a sugar-stick for the baby.

Willie Murray cut his thumb, couldn't count the damage,
Took the hide of an Ayrshire cow and used it for a bandage.
His brother caught three hundred cran when the seas were
    lavish,
Threw the bleeders back in the sea and went upon the parish.

It's no go the Herring Board, it's no go the Bible,
All we want is a packet of fags when our hands are idle.

It's no go the picture palace, it's no go the stadium,
It's no go the country cot with a pot of pink geraniums.
It's no go the Government grants, it's no go the elections,
Sit on your arse for fifty years and hang your hat on a pension.

It's no go my honey love, it's no go my poppet ;
Work your hands from day to day, the winds will blow the
    profit.
The glass is falling hour by hour, the glass will fall for ever,
But if you break the bloody glass you won't hold up the weather.

Les Sylphides

Life in a day : he took his girl to the ballet ;
Being shortsighted himself could hardly see it –
    The white skirts in the grey
    Glade and the swell of the music
    Lifting the white sails.

Calyx upon calyx, canterbury bells in the breeze
The flowers on the left mirror to the flowers on the right
    And the naked arms above
    The powdered faces moving
    Like seaweed in a pool.

Now, he thought, we are floating – ageless, oarless –
Now there is no separation, from now on
    You will be wearing white
    Satin and a red sash
    Under the waltzing trees.

But the music stopped, the dancers took their curtain,
The river had come to a lock – a shuffle of programmes –
    And we cannot continue down
    Stream unless we are ready
    To enter the lock and drop.

So they were married – to be the more together –
And found they were never again so much together,
    Divided by the morning tea,
    By the evening paper,
    By children and tradesmen's bills.

Waking at times in the night she found assurance
In his regular breathing but wondered whether
It was really worth it and where
The river had flowed away
And where were the white flowers.

Prayer Before Birth

I am not yet born; O hear me.
Let not the bloodsucking bat or the rat or the stoat or the
clubfooted ghoul come near me.

I am not yet born; console me.
I fear that the human race may with tall walls wall me,
with strong drugs dope me, with wise lies lure me,
on black racks rack me, in blood-baths roll me.

I am not yet born; provide me
With water to dandle me, grass to grow for me, trees to talk
to me, sky to sing to me, birds and a white light
in the back of my mind to guide me.

I am not yet born; forgive me
For the sins that in me the world shall commit, my words
when they speak me, my thoughts when they think me,
my treason engendered by traitors beyond me,
my life when they murder by means of my
hands, my death when they live me.

I am not yet born; rehearse me
In the parts I must play and the cues I must take when
old men lecture me, bureaucrats hector me, mountains
frown at me, lovers laugh at me, the white
waves call me to folly and the desert calls
me to doom and the beggar refuses
my gift and my children curse me.

I am not yet born; O hear me,
Let not the man who is beast or who thinks he is God
    come near me.

I am not yet born; O fill me
With strength against those who would freeze my
    humanity, would dragoon me into a lethal automaton,
        would make me a cog in a machine, a thing with
           one face, a thing, and against all those
               who would dissipate my entirety, would
                  blow me like thistledown hither and
                    thither or hither and thither
                      like water held in the
                        hands would spill me
Let them not make me a stone and let them not spill me.
Otherwise kill me.

W. H. AUDEN

Wystan Hugh Auden was born at York in 1907, the son of George Auden, M.D. and Constance Auden, and was educated at St Edmund's School, Grayshott, Gresham's School, Holt, and Christ Church, Oxford. After leaving the university he went to Berlin where he met Layard, psychologist and anthropologist, who

                  ... fed
   New doctrines into my receptive head.

     Part came from Lane, and part from D. H. Lawrence,
       Gide, though I didn't know it then, gave part.

The new doctrines can be found as a heavy deposit in Poems *(1930) and* The Orators *(1932), and more than traces of them survive even in Auden's most recent work* The Age of Anxiety *(1948). On his return from Germany Auden became a schoolmaster in England and Scotland before spending some time in documentary films – the verse commentary to* Night Mail, *made by the G.P.O. Film Unit,* is one result of this interest. 'Letter to Lord Byron' (Part IV) in Letters from Iceland (1937), a book written in collaboration with Louis MacNeice, is a short autobiography in verse up to the year 1936. Christopher Isherwood, who collaborated with Auden in three verse-plays (The Dog Beneath the Skin [1935], The Ascent of F6 [1936] and On the Frontier [1938]), as well as in a travel book about China, Journey to a War (1939), gives pictures of Auden at his prep. school and at Oxford in his autobiographical Lions and Shadows (1938). Auden himself has written about Gresham's School, Holt in The Old School, a symposium edited by Graham Greene.

During the Spanish Civil War Auden went to Spain and served as a stretcher-bearer and sanitary worker on the Republican side. He has travelled widely in continental Europe apart from visits (v. supra) to Iceland and China. In autumn, 1938, he went to the U.S.A. and is now permanently resident there. He has taught and lectured at various schools and universities in America, but now occupies himself entirely with writing. In 1937 Auden was awarded the King's Medal for Poetry in this country, and in 1945 he received the award of the American Academy of Arts and Letters. These are the only 'honours' I know of: no university in England has yet plucked up enough courage to offer him an honorary degree. During the last war he served with the Strategic Bombing Survey of the American Army in Germany, and he visited England for a short time in 1948.

Auden is an extremely prolific (and uneven) writer. Apart from the books and plays mentioned already, he had published before his departure to the U.S.A. the following works: The Dance of Death (1933) – drama; Look, Stranger! (1936) – poems; and two important anthologies, The Poet's Tongue (1935) – with John Garrett – and The Oxford Book of Light Verse (1938). Since that time he has issued the following collections of verse: Another Time (1940), New Year Letter (1941), For the Time Being (1945), and The Age of Anxiety (1948). The Auden double-number of New Verse contains a fairly complete list of Auden's writings up to November 1937 – this number should also be consulted for biographical details and some criticism – but there is no even moderately inclusive list

*known to me of the articles, reviews and introductions to books
written by Auden since 1938.*

*For criticism of Auden as a poet the reader should consult the files
of* New Verse, New Writing *and* Horizon. *There is a valuable
short note by Spender in* Poetry Since 1939 *and a study by Francis
Scarfe (whose article on the poet in* Auden and After, *1942, is
disappointing) entitled* Auden *(1948). I have not yet been able to
read this book. Both for its remarks on Auden and on other contemporary poets Geoffrey Grigson's excellent introduction to his
anthology,* Poetry of the Present *(1949) should be consulted. In
America mention may be made of the clever and perceptive but too
brightly written articles by the poet Randall Jarrell in the* Partisan
Review *(1945 and 1946).*

*The chief influence in the poetic movement of the 'thirties was, as
Spender says, undoubtedly the powerful intelligence and personality
of W. H. Auden, 'the most brilliant poet of his generation'.
Spender has characterized his work as 'the didactic, highly intellectualized, technically dazzling, at times wise poetry of an aloof
commentator', but this is not in my view the whole truth. Auden is
more involved in his subjects than this statement suggests, although
he is less involved than Spender himself, who tends to identify the
lyric with the subjective lyric and to carry the lyrical mood as far as
possible even into satirical and didactic writing. And, after all, it
was Auden's 'ice and wooden-faced acrobatics' which almost
persuaded Wyndham Lewis in the 'thirties that the poet was 'the
new guy who's got into the landscape'. Summing up, however,
Spender remarks that he thinks Auden has qualities of greatness.
With this I agree. As early as the collection* Look, Stranger!
*there are poems of astonishing truth and power. The sonnet
sequence, 'In Time of War', in* Journey to a War *seems to me
completely satisfying and quite free from the clevernesses, tricks
and obscurity of some of the earlier work. Since Auden left England
there have been persistent attempts to write him off, to suggest that
by so severing his roots his work has suffered in quality. I find these
attempts small-minded and silly and the conclusions drawn from his
departure absurd. In some of the later work Auden has certainly become more abstract as a result of new moral, philosophical and*

*religious interests – or, better, new emphasis on these old interests –
but the sequence 'The Quest' from* New Year Letter *is full of the
most extraordinary insight, and both* For The Time Being *and* The
Age of Anxiety *seem to me to contain long passages as brilliantly
conceived and as deftly written as anything he has done. There is
no space here to discuss his development from a 'political' to a 'religious' point of view – to speak thus for economy's sake is to use dangerous simplifications – but the reader keen to know more about the
matter is recommended to read in their chronological order Auden's
prose contributions to G. Grigson's* The Arts Today, *to the symposium* I Believe *(referred to in the note on MacNeice), and to
Stauffer's* The Intent of the Critic. *The last of these essays has been
reprinted in* The Mint *No. 2 (1948). He should then read the poems
again also in chronological order.*

*I think it true to say that no other poet writing in English to-day
has attempted as much as Auden; just as no other poet of his
generation can place beside his a body of work so exciting for its
peculiar insight, its range of reference and its skill in the use of
language and rhythm. In the variety of subjects and manners he
has used successfully, Auden has to be found a parallel outside
contemporary poetry altogether – in the painter Picasso.*

*I must omit the usual paragraph in explanation of my selections,
but for the understanding of 'Solo and Chorus' it is necessary to
point out that it is from the 'Annunciation' section of 'For The
Time Being', which has the sub-title 'a Christmas Oratorio'.*

From *The Dog Beneath the Skin*

Chorus

Happy the hare at morning, for she cannot read
The Hunter's waking thoughts. Lucky the leaf
Unable to predict the fall. Lucky indeed
The rampant suffering suffocating jelly
Burgeoning in pools, lapping the grits of the desert,
The elementary sensual cures,

The hibernations and the growth of hair assuage:
Or best of all the mineral stars disintegrating quietly into light.
Out what shall man do, who can whistle tunes by heart,
Know to the bar when death shall cut him short, like the cry of
    the shearwater?
We will show you what he has done.
How comely are his places of refuge and the tabernacles of his
    peace,
The new books upon the morning table, the lawns and the
    afternoon terraces!
Here are the playing-fields where he may forget his ignorance
To operate within a gentleman's agreement: twenty-two sins
    have here a certain licence.
Here are the thickets where accosted lovers combattant
May warm each other with their wicked hands,
Here are the avenues for incantation and workshops for the
    cunning engravers.
The galleries are full of music, the pianist is storming the keys,
    the great cellist is crucified over his instrument,
That none may hear the ejaculations of the sentinels
Nor the sigh of the most numerous and the most poor; the thud
    of their falling bodies
Who with their lives have banished hence the serpent and the
    faceless insect.

In Time of War

VIII

He turned his field into a meeting-place,
And grew the tolerant ironic eye,
And formed the mobile money-changer's face,
And found the notion of equality.

And strangers were as brothers to his clocks,
And with his spires he made a human sky;
Museums stored his learning like a box,
And paper watched his money like a spy.

It grew so fast his life was overgrown,
And he forgot what once it had been made for,
And gathered into crowds and was alone,

And lived expensively and did without,
And could not find the earth which he had paid for,
Nor feel the love that he knew all about.

Law, Say the Gardeners

Law, say the gardeners, is the sun,
Law is the one
All gardeners obey
To-morrow, yesterday, to-day.

Law is the wisdom of the old
The impotent grandfathers shrilly scold;
The grandchildren put out a treble tongue,
Law is the senses of the young.

Law, says the priest with a priestly look,
Expounding to an unpriestly people,
Law is the words in my priestly book,
Law is my pulpit and my steeple.

Law, says the judge as he looks down his nose.
Speaking clearly and most severely,
Law is as I've told you before,
Law is as you know I suppose,
Law is but let me explain it once more,
Law is The Law.

Yet law-abiding scholars write;
Law is neither wrong nor right,
Law is only crimes

Punished by places and by times,
Law is the clothes men wear
Anytime, anywhere,
Law is Good-morning and Good-night.

Others say, Law is our Fate;
Others say, Law is our State;
Others say, others say
Law is no more
Law has gone away.

And always the loud angry crowd
Very angry and very loud
Law is We,
And always the soft idiot softly Me.

If we, dear, know we know no more
Than they about the law,
If I no more than you
Know what we should and should not do
Except that all agree
Gladly or miserably
That the law is
And that all know this,
If therefore thinking it absurd
To identify Law with some other word,
Unlike so many men
I cannot say Law is again,
No more than they can we suppress
The universal wish to guess
Or slip out of our own position
Into an unconcerned condition.

Although I can at least confine
Your vanity and mine
To stating timidly
A timid similarity,

We shall boast anyway:
Like love I say.

Like love we don't know where or why
Like love we can't compel or fly
Like love we often weep
Like love we seldom keep.

The Quest

II

All had been ordered weeks before the start
From the best firms at such work; instruments
To take the measure of all queer events,
And drugs to move the bowels or the heart.

A watch, of course, to watch impatience fly,
Lamps for the dark and shades against the sun;
Foreboding, too, insisted on a gun,
And coloured beads to soothe a savage eye.

In theory they were sound on Expectation
Had there been situations to be in;
Unluckily they were their situation:

One should not give a poisoner medicine,
A conjurer fine apparatus, nor
A rifle to a melancholic bore.

From *New Year Letter*

I

A weary Asia out of sight
Is tugging gently at the night
Uncovering a restless race;

Clocks shoo the childhood from its face,
And accurate machines begin
To concentrate its adults in
A narrow day to exercise
Their gifts in some cramped enterprise.
How few pretend to like it: O,
Three-quarters of these people know
Instinctively what ought to be
The nature of society
And how they'd live there if they could.
If it were easy to be good,
And cheap, and plain as evil how,
We all would be its members now:
How readily would we become
The seamless live continuum
Of supple and coherent stuff
Whose form is truth, whose content love,
Its pluralist interstices
The homes of happiness and peace,
Where in a unity of praise
The largest publicum's a res
And the least res a publicum;
How grandly would our virtues bloom
In a more conscionable dust
Where Freedom dwells because it must
Necessity because it can,
And men confederate in Man.

But wishes are not horses: this
Annus is not Mirabilis;
Day breaks upon the world we know
Of war and wastefulness and woe,
Ashamed civilians come to grief
In brotherhoods without belief,
Whose good intentions cannot cure
The actual evils they endure
Nor smooth their practical career

Nor bring the far horizon near.
The New Year brings an earth afraid,
Democracy a ready-made
And noisy tradesman's slogan, and
The poor betrayed into the hand
Of lackeys with ideas, and truth
Whipped by their elders out of youth,
The peaceful fainting in their tracks
With martyrs' tombstones on their backs,
And culture on all fours to greet
A butch and criminal élite
While in the vale of silly sheep
Rheumatic old patricians weep.

II

O Unicorn among the cedars
To whom no magic charm can lead us,
White childhood moving like a sigh
Through the green woods unharmed in thy
Sophisticated innocence
To call thy true love to the dance;
O Dove of science and of light
Upon the branches of the night;
O Icthus playful in the keep
Sea-lodges that for ever keep
Their secret of excitement hidden;
O sudden Wind that blows unbidden
Parting the quiet reeds; O Voice
Within the labyrinth of choice
Only the passive listener hears;
O Clock and Keeper of the years;
O Source of equity and rest,
Quando non fuerit, non est,
It without image, paradigm
Of matter, motion, number, time,
The grinning gap of Hell, the hill
Of Venus and the stairs of Will,

Disturb our negligence and chill,
Convict our pride of its offence
In all things, even penitence,
Instruct us in the civil art
Of making from the muddled heart
A desert and a city where
The thoughts that have to labour there
May find locality and peace,
And pent-up feelings their release.
Send strength sufficient for our day,
And point our knowledge on its way,
O da quod jubes, Domine.

From *For the Time Being*

Solo and Chorus

Let number and weight rejoice
In this hour of their translation
Into conscious happiness:
For the whole in every part,
The truth at the proper centre
(*There's a Way. There's a Voice.*)
Of language and distress
Is recognized in her heart
Singing and dancing.

Let even the great rejoice.
Though buffeted by admirers
And arrogant as noon,
The rich and the lovely have seen
For an infinitesimal moment
(*There's a Way. There's a Voice.*)
In another's eye till their own
Reflection came between,
Singing and dancing.

Let even the small rejoice
Though threatened from purple rostra
And dazed by the soldier's drum
Proclaiming total defeat,
The general loquacious Public
(*There's a Way. There's a Voice.*)
Have been puzzled and struck dumb,
Hearing in every street
Singing and dancing.

Let even the young rejoice
Lovers at their betrayal
Weeping alone in the night,
Have fallen asleep as they heard,
Though too far off to be certain
(*There's a Way. There's a Voice.*)
They had not imagined it,
Sounds that made grief absurd,
Singing and dancing.

Let even the old rejoice
The Bleak and the Dim abandoned
By impulse and regret,
Are startled out of their lives;
For to footsteps long expected
(*There's a Way. There's a Voice.*)
Their ruins echo, yet
The Demolisher arrives
Singing and dancing.

JOHN LEHMANN

John Lehmann was born in June 1907 at Bourne End in the Thames Valley, and educated at Eton (King's Scholar) and Trinity College, Cambridge. He was the founder and editor of New Writing, *and he is now the managing director of the publishing house which bears his name, and editor of* Orpheus, *the miscellany replacing* New Writing. *(In parenthesis a glance at the first number of* Orpheus *and an early number of* New Writing *will supply a superficial but not false measure of the differences between the literary movements of the 'thirties and 'forties.) John Lehmann is also a brother of Rosamund Lehmann, the novelist, and Beatrix Lehmann, the actress. He has published several books of verse, of which the most recent (and, in my opinion, the best) are* Forty Poems *(1942) and* The Sphere of Glass *(1944). He has also written a novel, two books of travel and an informative critical study,* New Writing in Europe *(Pelican Books, 1940); and edited two anthologies,* Poems From New Writing *(1946) and* Shelley in Italy *(1947).*

'The Sphere of Glass' is reprinted from the volume of that name, I like it for its sobriety of feeling and the ease with which it moves.

The Sphere of Glass

So through the sun-laced woods they went
Where no one walked but two that day,
And they were poets, and content
Sharing the one deep-vistaed way,
Sister and brother, to walk on
Where years like thickets round them lay.

It was the Roman dyke that ran
Between the bluebells and the fern,
The loam so fresh, they half began
To feel the bones deep under turn,
And, listening, dreamed their argument
Something from ancient death would learn.

One bird among the golden-green
Spangle of leaves was poised to sing:
They heard the opening trill, and then
Silence; as if its heart could bring
No note so pure but would disturb
The soundless fountain of the Spring.

Within the wood, within that hour
It seemed a sphere of glass had grown
That glittered round their lives, with power
To link what grief the dyke had known
With voices of their vaster war
The sun-shot bombers' homing drone,

And make one tragic harmony
Where still this theme, their hope, returned,
And still the Spring unchangeably
In fires of its own sap was burned,
And poetry, from love and death,
The peace their human contest earned.

It might have been all history
Without the sphere of wonder lay
And just beyond their colloquy
Some truth more pure than they could say,
While through the bluebells and the fern
Sister and brother made their way.

KATHLEEN RAINE

Kathleen Raine was born in 1908 and educated at Girton College, Cambridge, where she specialized in biology and took her Natural Science Tripos in 1929. She contributed to New Verse in the 'thirties, but produced no collection until Stone and Flower (1943), a book illustrated with drawings by Barbara Hepworth. Her second book of verse, Living In Time, appeared in 1946, and her third, The Pythoness and Other Poems, in 1949. A concern with religion, not apparent in her earlier 'periodical' poems, is observable in Stone and Flower — see 'Prayer', 'Good Friday', etc. — and finds expression in 'Ecce Homo', one of the best poems in Living In Time. Generally speaking, Kathleen Raine is most at ease in the short lyric, and I have represented her by two lyrics, one from each of her two earlier books.

Passion

Full of desire I lay, the sky wounding me,
each cloud a ship without me sailing, each tree
possessing what my soul lacked, tranquillity.

Waiting for the longed-for voice to speak
through the mute telephone, my body grew weak
with the well-known and mortal death, heartbreak.

The language I knew best, my human speech
forsook my fingers, and out of reach
were Homer's ghosts, the savage conches of the beach.

Then the sky spoke to me in language clear,
familiar as the heart, than love more near.
The sky said to my soul, 'You have what you desire!

'Know now that you are born along with these
clouds, winds, and stars, and ever-moving seas
and forest dwellers. This your nature is.

Lift up your heart again without fear,
sleep in the tomb, or breathe the living air,
this world you with the flower and with the tiger share.'

Then I saw every visible substance turn
into immortal, every cell new born
burned with the holy fire of passion.

This world I saw as on her judgment day
when the war ends, and the sky rolls away,
and all is light, love and eternity.

The Spring

(Song)

Out of hope's eternal spring
Bubbled once my mountain stream
Moss and sundew, fern and fell,
Valley, summer, tree and sun
All rose up, and all are gone.

By the spring I saw my love
(All who have parted once must meet,
First we live, and last forget),
With the stars about his head
With the future in his heart
Lay the green earth at my feet.

Now by the spring I stand alone
Still are its singing waters flowing;
Oh never thought I here to greet
Shadowy death who comes this way
Where hope's waters rise and play!

STEPHEN SPENDER

Stephen Spender was born in February 1909, and educated at University College School, London, and University College, Oxford. At Oxford he was a contemporary of Auden and Mac-Neice, editing Oxford Poetry *with the latter in 1929 and with Bernard Spencer in 1930. On his mother's side he is partly of German descent, and his father, Harold Spender, was a Liberal writer and speaker. Spender went to Germany for a couple of years after leaving Oxford and he has since travelled widely in Europe. He was in Spain during the Civil War and did propaganda work for the Republicans. During the last war he was a fireman for a while in the N.F.S. in London and then (in his own words) 'a small hack of a war-time branch of the Foreign Office'.*

During the 'thirties Stephen Spender was a regular contributor to New Verse *and* New Writing, *and during the war he assisted Cyril Connolly to edit* Horizon. *The growth and development of his political opinions can be traced by reading first* Forward from Liberalism *(1937), which explores reasons for accepting Marxism as a working creed, and then* Life and the Poet *(1942), which finds better reasons for not doing so. 'I was always interested in politics', he wrote in* New Verse *in 1937, but I think it would be true to say that Spender's attachment to Communism derived less from an acceptance of dialectical materialism than from an active, angry pity for the underdog and an eager embracing of the Marxist millennial hope. In* Life and the Poet *he declares: 'the ultimate aim of politics is not politics, but the activities which can be practised within the political framework of the State. Therefore an effective statement of these activities — such as science, art, religion — is in itself a declaration of ultimate aims around which the political means will crystallize ... A society with no values outside politics is a machine carrying its human cargo, with no purpose in its institutions reflecting their cares, eternal aspirations, loneliness, need for love ...*' It is possible to present the change in Spender's views too dramatically, and perhaps he lends himself to this misrepresentation when he speaks in Poetry Since 1939 (*1946*) of the war compelling him to turn from outward events to search for 'a universal experience through subjective contemplation'. He is here referring to poems in Ruins and Visions (*1942*), but already in The Still Centre (*1939*) he had included a section of poems where '*I have deliberately turned back to a kind of writing which is more personal, and ... have included within my subjects weakness and fantasy and illusion.*' Apart from the books of verse mentioned Spender has written Poems (*1933*), Vienna (*1934*), Poems of Dedication (*1947*), The Edge of Being (*1949*) and the verse-play Trial of a Judge (*1938*).

With the exception of Auden, Spender is to me the most interesting poet of his generation and the one who seems most capable of further development. An exceptional, at times almost painful, honesty about himself and the world, allied to a very personal lyrical gift of expression, result in a tension in his work which gives the reader of it the sensation of walking through unfamiliar country where paradoxically the landmarks are all known. The poet is a co-discoverer with the reader, rather than a tutor (as Auden so often is). '*The Poetry is in the pity*' as often for Spender as for Wilfred Owen, and he has written movingly about elementary schoolchildren, the unemployed, the defeated in the Spanish Civil War. In spite of this I would describe his finest work as personal — for example the love-poems of '*A Separation*' (*Part I* of Ruins and Visions) and the sequence '*Elegy for Margaret*' in Poems of Dedication. Attention should also be drawn to '*Spiritual Explorations*' in the same volume. The second and third sonnets of this group rank with the best of Auden's sonnets in '*In Time of War*'.

Besides the books mentioned above Spender has also written short stories, a novel and much criticism. The Destructive Element (*1935*) contains his best critical prose, but all his literary criticism is worth reading a second time in spite of its uneven quality. There is an attractive and amusing glimpse of Spender in Isherwood's Lions and Shadows, *and the best article in Scarfe's* Auden and After *is devoted to him.*

'The Landscape Near an Aerodrome' is from the early Poems.
*It displays Spender's long, apparently careless, rhythmical breath,
his descriptive power, and his desire at this time to force his imagery
to point a moral (v. the last verse paragraph). 'Fall of a City' is
from the third part of* The Still Centre *'when I was preoccupied
with various kinds of political activity ... written directly and fairly
quickly from the experiences which suggested them'. 'The Double
Shame' is from Part I of* Ruins and Visions *and 'Elegy for
Margaret, IV' from* Poems of Dedication. *These groups of poems
have already been referred to in this note.*

The Landscape near an Aerodrome

More beautiful and soft than any moth
With burring furred antennae feeling its huge path
Through dusk, the air-liner with shut-off engines
Glides over suburbs and the sleeves set trailing tall
To point the wind. Gently, broadly, she falls
Scarcely disturbing charted currents of air.

Lulled by descent, the travellers across sea
And across feminine land indulging its easy limbs
In miles of softness, now let their eyes trained by watching
Penetrate through dusk the outskirts of this town
Here where industry shows a fraying edge.
Here they may see what is being done.

Beyond the winking masthead light
And the landing-ground, they observe the outposts
Of work: chimneys like lank black fingers
Or figures frightening and mad : and squat buildings
With their strange air behind trees, like women's faces
Shattered by grief. Here where few houses
Moan with faint light behind their blinds
They remark the unhomely sense of complaint, like a dog
Shut out and shivering at the foreign moon.

In the last sweep of love, they pass over fields
Behind the aerodrome, where boys play all day
Hacking dead grass : whose cries, like wild birds,
Settle upon the nearest roofs
But soon are hid under the loud city.

Then, as they land, they hear the tolling bell
Reaching across the landscape of hysteria
To where, larger than all the charcoaled batteries
And imaged towers against that dying sky,
Religion stands, the church blocking the sun.

Fall of a City

All the posters on the walls
All the leaflets in the streets
Are mutilated, destroyed or run in rain,
Their words blotted out with tears,
Skins peeling from their bodies
In the victorious hurricane.

All the names of heroes in the hall
Where the feet thundered and the bronze throats roared,
FOX and LORCA claimed as history on the walls,
Are now angrily deleted
Or to dust surrender their dust,
From golden praise excluded.

All the badges and salutes
Torn from lapels and from hands
Are thrown away with human sacks they wore
Or in the deepest bed of mind
They are washed over with a smile
Which launches the victors when they win.

All the lessons learned, unlearnt;
The young, who learned to read, now blind
Their eyes with an archaic film;
The peasant relapses to a stumbling tune
Following the donkey's bray;
These only remember to forget.

But somewhere some word presses
On the high door of a skull, and in some corner
Of an irrefrangible eye
Some old man's memory jumps to a child
– Spark from the days of energy.
And the child hoards it like a bitter toy.

The Double Shame

You must live through the time when everything hurts
When the space of the ripe, loaded afternoon
Expands to a landscape of white heat frozen
And trees are weighed down with hearts of stone
And green stares back where you stare alone,
And the walking eyes throw flinty comments
And the words which carry most knives are the blind
Phrases searching to be kind.

Solid and usual objects are ghosts
The furniture carries cargoes of memory,
The staircase has corners which remember
As fire blows red in gusty embers,
And each empty dress cuts out an image
In fur and evening and summer and gold
Of her who was different in each.

Pull down the blind and lie on the bed
And clasp the hour in the glass of one room
Against your mouth like a crystal doom.

Take up the book and look at the letters
Hieroglyphs on sand and as meaningless –
Here birds crossed once and cries were uttered
In a mist where sight and sound are blurred.

For the story of those who made mistakes
Of one whose happiness pierced like a star
Eludes and evades between sentences
And the letters break into eyes which read
What the blood is now writing in your head,
As though the characters sought for some clue
To their being so perfectly living and dead
In your story, worse than theirs, but true.

Set in the mind of their poet, they compare
Their tragic bliss with your trivial despair
And they have fingers which accuse
You of the double way of shame.
At first you did not love enough
And afterwards you loved too much
And you lacked the confidence to choose
And you have only yourself to blame.

Elegy for Margaret

IV

Poor girl, inhabitant of a strange land
Where death stares through your gaze,
As though a distant moon
Shone through midsummer days
With the skull-like glitter of night:

Poor child, you wear your summer dress
And your shoes striped with gold
As the earth wears a variegated cover
Of grass and flowers
Covering caverns of destruction over
Where hollow deaths are told.

I look into your sunk eyes,
Shafts of wells to both our hearts,
Which cannot take part in the lies
Of acting these gay parts.
Under our lips, our minds
Become one with the weeping
Of the mortality
Which through sleep is unsleeping.

Of what use is my weeping?
It does not carry a surgeon's knife
To cut the wrongly multiplying cells
At the root of your life.
It can only prove
That extremes of love
Stretch beyond the flesh to hideous bone
Howling in hyena dark alone.

Oh, but my grief is thought, a dream,
Tomorrow's gale will sweep away.
It does not wake every day
To the facts which are and do not only seem:
The granite facts around your bed,
Poverty-stricken hopeless ugliness
Of the fact that you will soon be dead.

W. R. RODGERS

W. R. Rodgers was born in Ulster in 1909 and educated at Queen's University, Belfast. After twelve years spent as a clergyman in County Armagh, he resigned his parish in 1946 and joined the B.B.C. Features Department in London. His only collection of verse, Awake! and Other Poems, *was published in 1941 (after a first printing in 1940 had been entirely destroyed by enemy action), but his poems continue to appear in literary magazines. He began to write poetry rather late. 'I was schooled,' he explains, 'in a backwater of literature out of sight of the running stream of contemporary verse. Some rumours of course I heard, but I was singularly ignorant of its extent and character. It was in the late 'thirties that I came to contemporary poetry, and I no longer stood dumb in the tied shops of speech or felt stifled in the stale air of convention.'*

Awake! and Other Poems *attracted attention on its publication and several reviewers spoke of it as the most promising first book of poetry since Auden's* Poems. *Although I appreciate Rodgers's work, I cannot accept this opinion. The influence of the technique of Hopkins is apparent in the bold alliteration and sometimes in the speed of movement, as the influence of Auden is felt in the use of personification (v. 'End of a World', for example), but it may be questioned whether these are good influences. 'Hopkinese', in particular, does not export well. It was tailored by Hopkins for his own purposes, and, worn by anyone else, it has a reach-me-down effect. Generally Rodgers's use of language is individual: he has at beck and call a wide vocabulary which he deploys with an Irish exuberance. His subject-matter is the appearances of things rendered vividly and directly – in a manner that sometimes reminds us of MacNeice – with a quick eye for the arresting detail. 'Summer Holidays' with its fluency, its neat observation and its long conveyor-belt of 'story' illustrates most of his virtues as a poet and one obvious weakness: the rather commonplace ideas which have been organized for expression by his observation and technical skill.*

'Stormy Day' *and* *'Life's Circumnavigators'* *are from* Awake! *and*
Other Poems. *The later poems show a refinement of technique, but*
no other development. This judgment may sound severe, but how
much better Rodgers writes than the neo-romantics of the 'forties.

Stormy Day

O look how the loops and balloons of bloom
Bobbing on long strings from the finger-ends
And knuckles of the lurching cherry-tree
Heap and hug, elbow and part, this wild day,
Like a careless carillon cavorting;
And the beaded whips of the beeches splay
And dip like anchored weed round a drowned rock,
And hovering effortlessly the rooks
Hang on the wind's effrontery as if
On hooks, then loose their hold and slide away
Like sleet sidewards down the warm swimming sweep
Of wind. O it is a lovely time when
Out of the sunk and rigid sumps of thought
Our hearts rise and race with new sounds and sights
And signs, tingling delightedly at the sting
And crunch of springless carts on gritty roads,
The caught kite dangling in the skinny wires,
The swipe of a swallow across the eyes,
Striped awnings stretched on lawns. New things surprise
And stop us everywhere. In the parks
The fountains scoop and flower like rockets
Over the oval ponds whose even skin
Is pocked and goosefleshed by their niggling rain
That frocks a naked core of statuary.
And at jetty's jut, roped and ripe for hire,
The yellow boats lie yielding and lolling,
Jilted and jolted like jellies. But look!
There! Do you see, crucified on palings,

Motionless news-posters announcing
That now the frozen armies melt and meet
And smash? Go home now, for, try as you may,
You will not shake off that fact to-day.
Behind you limps that dog with tarry paw,
As behind him, perfectly-timed, follows
The dumb shadow that mimes him all the way.

Life's Circumnavigators

Here, where the taut wave hangs
Its tented tons, we steer
Through rocking arch of eye
And creaking reach of ear,
Anchored to flying sky,
And chained to changing fear.

O when shall we, all spent,
Row in to some far strand,
And find, to our content,
The original land
From which our boat once went,
Though not the one we planned.

Us on that happy day
This fierce sea will release,
On our rough face of clay,
The final glaze of peace.
Our oars we all will lay
Down, and desire will cease.

BERNARD SPENCER

Bernard Spencer was born in 1909 and educated at Marlborough and Corpus Christi College, Oxford. He was twice editor of Oxford Poetry *and, after leaving the university, for a number of years worked as a schoolmaster, then on film-scripts and in an advertising agency. Since 1941 he has lectured for the British Council in Greece, Egypt and Italy, and he has also done talks on travel and literature for the B.B.C. At present he is at the British Institute in Turin.*

Many of his earlier poems were published in New Verse, *which he helped Geoffrey Grigson to edit in the late 'thirties, and between 1942 and 1945 he did a similar job (with Lawrence Durrell and Robin Fedden) for* Personal Landscape, *the poetry magazine in the Middle East. His only book of verse is* Aegean Islands (1946), *but he has also edited (with Durrell and Nanos Valoritis) a book of translations from modern Greek,* The King of Asine.

'Allotments: April' *was first published in* New Verse *in 1936 and 'On the Road' in* Penguin New Writing *in 1947. Both seem to me to have an unpretentious clarity and directness and to be good poems. 'Allotments: April' might very well represent the kind of poem for which* New Verse *stood: straightforward but unpedestrian language, feeling expressed through observation, intelligence reflecting on observation and awake to the implications of feeling. Like other* New Verse *poets Bernard Spencer was influenced by Auden, Spender and MacNeice. He had mild left-wing sympathies in the 'thirties — these come out in a few poems — but was not really of a political temper at all. His love poems in the 'thirties and 'forties seem to me his best pieces.*

Allotments: April

Cobbled with rough stone which rings my tread
The path twists through the squared allotments.
Blinking to glimpse the lark in the warming sun,
In what sense am I joining in
Such a hallooing, rousing April day,
Now that the hedges are so gracious and
Stick out at me moist buds, small hands, their opening scrolls
    and fans?

Lost to some of us the festival joy
At the bursting of the tomb, the seasonal mystery,
God walking again who lay all winter
As if in those long barrows built in the fields
To keep the root-crops warm. On squires' lawns
The booted dancers twirl. But what I hear
Is spade slice in pebbled earth swinging the nigger-coloured
    loam.

And the love-songs, the mediaeval grace,
The fluting lyrics, 'The only pretty ring-time',
These have stopped singing. For love detonates like sap
Up into the limbs of men and bears all the seasons
And the starving and the cutting and hunts terribly through
    lives
To find its peace. But April comes as
Beast-smell flung from the fields, the hammers, the loud-
    speaking weir.

The rough voices of boys playing by the hedge,
As manly as possible, their laughter, the big veins
Sprawled over the beet-leaf, light-red fires
Of flower pots heaped by the huts; they make a pause in
The wireless voice repeating pacts, persecutions,
And imprisonments and deaths and heaped violent deaths,
Impersonal now as figures in the city news.

Behind me, the town curves. Its parapeted edge,
With its burnt look, guards towards the river,
The worry about money, the eyeless work
Of those who do not believe, real poverty,
The sour doorways of the poor; April which
Delights the trees and fills the roads to the South,
Does not deny or conceal. Rather it adds

What more I am; excites the deep glands
And warms my animal bones as I go walking
Past the allotments and the singing water-meadows
Where hooves of cattle have plodded and cratered, and
Watch to-day go up like a single breath
Holding in its applause at masts of height
Two elms and their balanced attitude like dancers,
    their arms like dancers.

On the Road

Our roof was grapes and the broad hands of the vine
as we two drank in the vine-chinky shade
of harvest France;
and wherever the white road led we could not care,
it had brought us there
to the arbour built on a valley side where time,
if time any more existed, was that river
of so profound a current, it at once
both flowed and stayed.

We two. And nothing in the whole world was lacking.
It is later one realizes. I forget
the exact year or what we said. But the place
for a lifetime glows with noon. There are the rustic
table and the benches set; beyond the river
forests as soft as fallen clouds, and in

our wine and eyes I remember other noons.
It is a lot to say, nothing was lacking;
river, sun and leaves, and I am making
words to say 'grapes' and 'her skin'.

RAYNER HEPPENSTALL

*Rayner Heppenstall was born in Huddersfield in 1911 and educated,
as he says, 'at public elementary schools and in the back streets'.
He went on to secondary schools and to the universities of Leeds and
Strasbourg. He became a schoolmaster, but was sacked after teaching for seven months, and then took to book illustration, lecturing
and literary journalism. Weakness of eyesight caused him to consider the problem of blindness, and this led to the writing of* The
Blaze of Noon. *During the war he served in the army. Since then
he has worked for the B.B.C. as a producer and has written and
produced many feature programmes. He has also written a good
deal of critical prose particularly on modern French literature (see also his useful introduction to Guido de Ruggiero's*
Existentialism), *and has published the following books of poetry:*
First Poems (*1935*), Sebastian (*1937*), Blind Men's Flowers are
Green (*1940*). Poems 1933–1945 (*1946*) *collects what the author
wishes to preserve from these volumes and adds two short poems.
'Moon' is the last poem of a sequence on 'The Planets', originally
published in* Blind Men's Flowers are Green.

*In my opinion Rayner Heppenstall is (like Herbert Read) a
critic of intelligence with a real sensitivity to words, rarely a satisfactory poet.* Poems 1933–1945 *contains much polished and some
subtle writing, but only a handful of genuine poems. 'Moon' is one
of these.*

From *The Planets*

Moon

With swollen visage, eyes red and full of water,
Round the equator she drags tides and herself,
Herself tied down by gravitational order

By this earth's gravity held which, if she left
Her vaulted suffocation, should indeed falter
And all its crystalline death and spirits therein

Rend and be free and no man born of the moon
Groan in his mineral blindness. It is her nature
Upon this powerful invocation to give you

Silver the blood of the poor in a ring of rain,
And she has friends, beside a few minds of her quality,
Land-Snail and shell-fish as well as fish and the frog.

As well as the hare, the swan and the nightingale.

FRANCIS SCARFE

Francis Scarfe was born in 1911 and educated at King's College, Durham University, and Fitzwilliam House, Cambridge. He has also studied at the Sorbonne. For a time he was a supervisor in French at Trinity College, Cambridge, and later an assistant master at the Collège Chaptal in Paris. Before the war he became a lecturer in French at Glasgow University, and has now returned there after war service in the army (educational work in the Orkneys and Faroes) and peace service in adult education for Oxford University. He gives some details of himself and his attitude to poetry in his Auden and After *(1942), but the book was too quickly written after insufficient consideration, and it is probable that Scarfe would wish to withdraw some of the statements made there. He has published several books of verse from the Fortune Press and made several translations, including a recent one of Valéry's* La Jeune Parque, *but he wishes his poetry to be judged by his* Collected Poems *to be issued by Poetry London in 1950.*

'Tyne Dock', reprinted from The Listener, *is a piece of auto-biographical nostalgia, unequal, like much of Scarfe's work, but emotionally honest. Spender has praised Scarfe's work for its honesty and sensitivity. It is possible that he finds something of his own manner there, for Scarfe inclines to think that the poetic gifts possessed by Spender are the most important ones.*

Tyne Dock

The summer season at Tyne Dock
Lifted my boyhood in a crane
Above the shaggy mining town,
Above the slaghills and the rocks,
Above the middens in backlanes
And wooden hen-huts falling down.

Grass grew vermilion in the streets
Where the blind pit-ponies pranced
And poppies screamed by butchers' stalls
Where bulls kicked sparks with dying feet,
And in the naked larks I sensed
A cruel god beneath it all.

Over the pithead wheel the moon
Was clean as a girl's face in school;
I envied the remote old man
Who lived there, quiet and alone,
While in the kitchen the mad spool
Unwound, as Annie's treadle ran.

The boyish season is still there
For clapping hands and leaping feet
Across the slagheaps and the dunes,
And still it breaks into my care
Though I will never find the street,
Nor find the old, impulsive tune,
Nor ever lose that child's despair.

CHARLES MADGE

Charles Madge was born at Johannesburg, South Africa, in 1912 and educated at Winchester and Magdalene College, Cambridge. After a year in Fleet Street as a reporter, he helped to found Mass Observation. Later he did social and economic research under the guidance of Lord Keynes and for P.E.P. He was a director of the Pilot Press for three years and edited Pilot Papers. *He is now Social Development Officer for the new Stevenage. His publications include two collections of verse:* The Disappearing Castle *(1937)* and The Father Found *(1941).*

In approaching Charles Madge's work it is useful to remember two things: that he went to Cambridge and is an admirer of William Empson; and that political sympathies brought him for a time under the influence of the 'social' poets of the 'thirties — there are early Audenesque verses by Madge in Michael Roberts's New Country *(1933), and he was a regular contributor to* New Verse. *Madge is often an obscure poet (like Empson) in the sense that he does not seem to be caring very much whether the reader is following him, and he uses scientific references, not in Auden's popular way, but accurately and professionally. Yet it would give a false impression to imply that his work is generally obscure, or that it has anything like the same degree of complication as Empson's. 'Loss' from* The Father Found *is fairly representative. It uses a metrical pattern which Empson might have chosen, opens with a scientific image —*

Like the dark germs across the filter clean

– then moves on to speak of *Vienna* and its '*wounded walls*', a reference to the bombardment of the workers' flats. *Again, apart from the social poets and Cambridge, it is useful to bear in mind Madge's interest in the literature of the quarter-century preceding the Romantic Revival. The sequence* '*Delusions*' *would hardly have been written without Gray. In Madge's first volume the short pieces* '*In Conjunction*', '*Fortune*' *and* '*Solar Creation*' (*which is particularly fine*) *have been appreciated, and there are pieces with a similar appeal in* The Father Found. *One trouble for the anthologist is that Madge has definite ideas about his best poems, and has failed to collect, and refuses to allow to be reprinted, certain pieces which now disappoint him, e.g.* '*Drawing Room Experience*', (The Year's Poetry, 1938). *This is a poem I find, perhaps wrongly, very attractive.*

'*Ode*' *is from* The Father Found. '*Inscription I*', *a recent uncollected poem, is more typical of his imagery and rhythms.*

Ode

The lesson of our time is sore
Having and to have no more,
Within the smoky reference
Of life and its indifference.

Whether in want, whether in wealth,
There is no peace, there is no health.
To enact the plot we're fated
In the world that we've created.

The innumerable heart-beats
Of the traffic and the streets,
The impassive architecture
And the whole colossal structure

But elaborately disguise
Confusion and the nest of spies:
Always the policeman stands
With the baton in his hands.

Those from whom the industrial vulture
Draws the sinews of its culture,
For whom the evil choice is small,
If it is a choice at all,

Badly housed, badly fed
And abominably misled,
In the lottery of life
Can lose a job or choose a wife.

Those who love the time of play
Or to drink the time away
Or the curls and smiles that vie
In the wineshop of the eye

May win bitterness and pain
May win happiness again
And from the nature of the odds
Authenticate their various gods.

Still the million fires burn
Still the million souls can learn,
Ever loving and reviling,
Hating and then reconciling,

Ever finding and concealing
The diversity of feeling,
Life is irretrievable
But death is inconceivable.

Inscription I

Here cries chisel-parted stone
High, dry and wingless.

In hollow warning like the moon
Her own appearing ghost.

The wind blows, the wind blows away
From the small piping glottis
Words, airy and small
The wind blows, the wind blows away
Scuttering messages into darkness
And among muffled feet

But these remain from time again
Departed relatives
Ignored, yet they persist
And will not easily dissolve
In the hard rain and gentle rain.

These had a resonance, it seems
An engram, as a leaf
Is mottled in its fall.
They cut them square, as though they did not feel,
And finding nature, left a line,
Line upon line, a pale and crooked line
The shadowless wall people

Good grooves for lichen spores and chance connections.

HENRY TREECE

Henry Treece was born in the Midlands in 1912, but is of Welsh origin. He was educated at Birmingham University (where he was Captain of Boxing) before becoming a schoolmaster. At various times he has also been a university extension lecturer, an artists' model and a pianist in a dance band. When war broke out he became an A.R.P. Control Room Officer and later a pilot-officer in the R.A.F.V.R. With J. F. Hendry he was joint-leader of the Apocalyptic movement in contemporary literature, and he was co-editor of the two Apocalyptic anthologies –The New Apocalypse (1939) *and* The White Horseman (1941).

The Apocalyptic movement, which may now be said to be dead (if one is generous enough to admit that it was ever alive), was a reaction against political elements in the literature of the 'thirties and, more particularly, a reaction against 'social reporting' in poetry. The movement had negative political and social aims, disclaiming any political allegiance to existing groups, disliking the machine-age, and calling loudly for a revival of myth. Literary ancestors of the movement – this was in imitation of some of the sweeping claims of the Surrealists – were said to be the author of the Book of Revelation, Shakespeare, Webster, Blake and Kafka, a suspiciously miscellaneous crew. None of this would have mattered had the Apocalyptics included a few real poets and short-story writers. Names associated with the movement were those of J. F. Hendry, Nicholas Moore, Tom Scott, Norman McCaig and G. S. Fraser. These were writers of talent – specimens of the work of most of them can be found in M. J. Tambimuttu's Poetry in Wartime (1942) *– but the body of verse produced by them (with the exception of G. S. Fraser's work) seems to me tame, second-hand and sometimes derivative; and it is often difficult to see why it should be called Apocalyptic. I have not included these poets in this anthology. Instead I have represented the movement by a single poem by Henry Treece, who seems to me the most accomplished of*

its 'typical' writers, although I do not like what he is trying to do
and find myself repelled by the touch of whimsy in many of his pieces.

'Legend' is reprinted from the section 'Mystic Numbers' of
Invitation and Warning.

Legend

There was a man
With a coloured coat of rags
Who left his body and blood on a tree.
But the thieves at his side gave the bones to the dogs,
And the black-thorn cock sang merrily.

The lads of the town
Drank down to the dregs
Then took a sharp axe to lop the tree.
But the thieves had been there first gathering logs,
And the black-thorn cock sang steadily.

One day at dawn
Upon their nags
Twelve tinkers came and their hearts were free,
For they cut twelve whistles from the knuckles of the dogs,
To bear the black cock company.

ANNE RIDLER

Anne Bradby was born in 1912 at Rugby, where her father and
uncle were housemasters of Rugby School. In 1938 she married
Vivian Ridler and is now the mother of two daughters and a son.
She has published one main collection of poems, The Nine Bright
Shiners (1943) – this was preceded by smaller collections, Poems
and A Dream Observed – and two verse-plays, Cain (1944) and
The Shadow Factory (1946), the latter produced by Martin

Browne in his season of plays by poets at the Mercury Theatre. She has a new book, Henry Bly and Other Plays, *in preparation. Anne Ridler has also edited* Shakespeare Criticism 1919–35 *and* A Little Book of Modern Verse (*in my opinion the best of the shorter anthologies*).

The subjects of Mrs Ridler's poems are domestic and religious, so that it was inevitable that some critics would talk of Patmore, particularly as she has intelligence and a verbal wit expressing itself with the utmost neatness rhythmically. To Focus Three, *a symposium on T. S. Eliot, she contributed an excellent article, 'A Question of Speech', from which I extract the following:*

> *For myself, I should say it was Eliot who first made me despair of becoming a poet; Auden (with, of course, dead poets, notably Sir Thomas Wyatt) who first made me think I saw how to become one.*
>
> *An age can afford a few good poets who stand aside from this battle for the colloquial idiom in poetry, and continue to use the artificial diction of an earlier generation – as, in our own day, are such diverse poets as Walter de la Mare and Charles Williams – but not many; and with these, the young must 'admire and do otherwise', as Hopkins put it. It can also afford a different kind of poet, who treats words as though he were present at their creation – a Dylan Thomas or a George Barker – but only if the main channel is kept clear. These are the luxury of a strong tradition.*

At Parting

Since we through war awhile must part
Sweetheart, and learn to lose
Daily use
Of all that satisfied our heart:
Lay up those secrets and those powers
Wherewith you pleased and cherished me these two years:

Now we must draw, as plants would,
On tubers stored in a better season,

Our honey and heaven;
Only our love can store such food.
Is this to make a god of absence?
A new-born monster to steal our sustenance?

We cannot quite cast out lack and pain.
Let him remain – what he may devour
We can well spare:
He never can tap this, the true vein.
I have no words to tell you what you were,
But when you are sad, think, Heaven could give no more.

For a Child Expected

Lovers whose lifted hands are candles in winter,
Whose gentle ways like streams in the easy summer,
Lying together
For secret setting of a child, love what they do,
Thinking they make that candle immortal, those streams forever
        flow,
And yet do better than they know.

So the first flutter of a baby felt in the womb,
Its little signal and promise of riches to come,
Is taken in its father's name;
Its life is the body of his love, like his caress,
First delicate and strange, that daily use
Makes dearer and priceless.

Our baby was to be the living sign of our joy,
Restore to each the other's lost infancy;
To a painter's pillaging eye
Poet's coiled hearing, add the heart we might earn
By the help of love; all that our passion would yield
We put to planning our child.

The world flowed in; whatever we liked we took:
For its hair, the gold curls of the November oak
We saw on our walk;
Snowberries that make a Milky Way in the wood
For its tender hands; calm screen of the frozen flood
For our care of its childhood.

But the birth of a child is an uncontrollable glory;
Cat's cradle of hopes will hold no living baby,
Long though it lay quietly.
And when our baby stirs and struggles to be born
It compels humility: what we began
Is now its own.

For *as the sun that shines through glass*
So Jesus in His Mother was.
Therefore every human creature,
Since it shares in His nature,
In candle-gold passion or white
Sharp star should show its own way of light.
May no parental dread or dream
Darken our darling's early beam:
May she grow to her right powers
Unperturbed by passion of ours.

KENNETH ALLOTT

Kenneth Allott was born in 1912 and educated at various schools and at the universities of Durham and Oxford. He has worked as a journalist, a schoolmaster and a staff tutor in adult education, and is now a Lecturer in English Literature at Liverpool University. He was a regular contributor to New Verse, *and, for a time, assistant editor. He is the author of a novel, a biography of Jules Verne and two collections of poems –* Poems *(1938) and* The Ventriloquist's Doll *(1943) – and he has published a critical edition of William Habington's poems.* A Room With a View, *a play adapted from E. M. Forster's novel of the same name by Kenneth Allott and Stephen Tait, was performed at the Cambridge Arts Theatre in February 1950. He has also completed a study of Graham Greene's novels to be published shortly, and he has a biography of Matthew Arnold in preparation.*

'The Memory of Yeats' and 'Two Ages' are reprinted from The Ventriloquist's Doll.

The Memory of Yeats

O mirror which time unsilvers now, now
That the clocks stop, ormulu or gilt glassy Victorian
Between black ferns, now that the Parthenon
Shudders and disintegrates into secular dust,
And all the libraries of the great are fallen,
And one last acid wave
Washes and scoops mind's cave and leaves it to oblivion;

O sea-wracked, lost before the wax of the Purification
With the wild voices off the slushy streets,
With the gas lit in the office afternoon
Hissing hatred from a faulty mantle
Like a fish garrotted in air;
O heart's confessional, buried in a bitter winter
Before crocus or snowdrop
When water of war crept higher,
The tears to flow in many a prefecture
From submarine cisterns of loss and revenge;
You, who were taken from us before the snow,
How will it be with us now?

'*A bas les aristos!*' but who now will scratch
The eyes of the hateful Bethel, babbling texts,
Or assault the backside of the Saxon ruin
Waving its cheque-book by St George's Channel,
Or sorrow again as when the Irish made
Their Easter duty of rebellion?

Never a bomb in railway waiting-room
Shall speak as you spoke from a round tower
Of pride and minstrelsy. The regalia of power
Are buried centuries deep, and dead the throaty music of the
    swan:
You have emigrated like all Irishmen.

For the voice modulating through seven heavens, more potent
    than poteen,
Prince of bushido reared where the staple potato
Furnishes the illicit still with political magic
And the cotton-plant and bog-auricula
Weep on moss under the coasting buzzard;
Where the platonic weapon of the blackthorn shillelagh
Stammers its Erse among cromlechs and Celtic crosses
With snake-charming Patrick and a hundred masses
Per diem for the souls in purgatory –
He will not return this anniversary.

He will not return this anniversary
Though Shannon light a hundred thousand lamps
Burning a brogue of gaiety and heart-lore
While seminaries fondle the syllogism
In their crepuscular Holy Ghostliness
(Darii, Celarent, Ferio and Barbara);
Though Ulster like an amputated limb
In its north of flax and shipyards bickers to enlistment,
In its baffled basalt and steam-hammers' clangour:
For The Harp That Once will not sound any more.

O western non-pareil, grieve not to be
Never to grieve again, never to hear
The owls of midnight in the hazel-wood,
Or see first smoke rising from a waking city
In summer when the amazing fuchsia
Is resonant yet with the top-heavy bee;
For you belong to the freemasonry

Of the rising peat-drenched wind and robber sea
Of winter. No more have you to fear
The minatory tongue of the mad partisan
Or howling schoolroom recitation.
You are enfranchised of destroying pity;
You are elect to linger here
As man and myth
As long as our intemperate literature.

Two Ages

Ballet of Fahrenheit and Réaumur,
The swarm of bees round time's thermometer,
The Sheffield edge of summer where,
Baffled at every cardinal point with cuckoos,
Sturdy as dandelion, tanned juventus
Straddles on river-bank to arch his piss
Into a rainbow cataract of sun,
Ears pricked for sexual music, view-halloos
To a death-brush with sense
So glittering, so glittering
After the glory-leap down the ravine.
He may be happy even once,
Or think he is,
Away from home's maternal echoes,
As innocent as a clock
Before time's shipwreck.

But when the rowdy summer is kaput
And birds must emigrate
From unfond headlands; when skies shiver
To stream blind windows and to raise gooseflesh
And everything is over:
He will transmogrify the wish
And set up house

And burn his own coal in the hearth
And have a good address
Religiously for ever;
Prefer the sun's low course,
Creating his own snow,
A walking Greenland now,
To his own children marking good and evil,
Becoming his own devil,
As usual, as usual.

F. T. PRINCE

Frank Templeton Prince was born at Kimberley in 1912 and educated at schools in South Africa and at Balliol College, Oxford. He did some literary research in America before 1939 and, during the war, became a captain in the Intelligence Corps. He is now a Lecturer in English Literature at University College, Southampton. His only book of verse, Poems, *was published in 1938.*

F. T. Prince is not a writer who seeks the limelight or is ever likely to become a nine days' wonder as other modern poets, good and bad, have done and, doubtless, will do. Stephen Spender, who first pointed out his merits to me in 1938, speaks of him in Poetry Since 1939 *as 'one of the finest young poets now writing in English'.*

'Soldiers Bathing' is uncollected, but it has been printed in several anthologies. The version given here incorporates the writer's latest improvements and corrections.

Soldiers Bathing

The sea at evening moves across the sand,
And under a sunset sky I watch the freedom of a band
Of soldiers who belong to me: stripped bare
For bathing in the sea, they shout and run in the warm air.

Their flesh, worn by the trade of war, revives
And watching them, my mind towards the meaning of it strives.

All's pathos now. The body that was gross,
Rank, ravening, disgusting in the act and in repose,
All fever, filth and sweat, all bestial strength
And bestial decay, by pain and labour grows at length
Fragile and luminous. 'Poor bare forked animal',
Conscious of his desires and needs and flesh that rise and fall,
Stands in the soft air, tasting after toil
The sweetness of his nakedness: letting the sea-waves coil
Their frothy tongues about his feet, forgets
His hatred of the war, its terrible pressure that begets
A machinery of death and slavery,
Each being a slave and making slaves of others: finds that he
Remembers his old freedom in a game
Mocking himself, and comically mimics fear and shame.

He plays with death and animality,
And reading in the shadows of his pallid flesh, I see
The idea of Michelangelo's cartoon
Of soldiers bathing, breaking off before they were half done
At some sortie of the enemy, an episode
Of the Pisan wars with Florence. I remember how he showed
Their muscular limbs that clamber from the water
And heads that turn across the shoulder, eager for the slaughter,
Forgetful of their bodies that are bare,
And hot to buckle on and use the weapons lying there.
And I think too of the theme another found
When, shadowing lean bodies on a sinister red ground –
Was it Antonio Pollaiuolo? –
Painted a naked battle: warriors straddled, hacked the foe,
Dug their bare toes into the soil and slew
The brother-naked man who lay between their feet and drew
His lips back from his teeth in a grimace.

They were Italians who knew war's sorrow and disgrace
And showed the thing suspended, stripped, a theme
Born out of the experience of war's horrible extreme
Beneath a sky where even the air flows
With *Lachrimae Christi;* and that rage, that bitterness, those
    blows,
That hatred of the slain, what could it be
But indirectly or brutally a commentary
On the Crucifixion? for the picture burns
With indignation and pity and despair and love by turns
Because it is the obverse of the scene
Where Christ hangs murdered, stripped, upon the Cross:
    I mean,
That is the explanation of its rage.

And we too have our bitterness and pity that engage
Thought, horror in this war. But night begins,
Night of the mind: who nowadays is conscious of our sins?
Though every human deed concerns our blood,
And even we must know what no one yet has understood,
That some great love is over what we do,
And that is what has driven us to this fury, for so few
Can suffer all the terror of that love:
The terror of that love has set us spinning in this groove
Greased with our blood.

              These dry themselves and dress,
Resume their shirts, forget the fear and shame of nakedness.
Because to love is frightening we prefer
The freedom of our crimes. Yet as I drink the dusky air,
I feel a strange delight that fills me full,
A gratitude, as if evil itself were beautiful;
And kiss the wound in thought, while in the west
I watch a streak of red that might have issued from Christ's
    breast.

ROY FULLER

Roy Fuller was born in 1912 at Oldham, Lancashire. He served in the Royal Navy from 1941 to 1946, most of the time in the Fleet Air Arm. In civilian life he is a solicitor. He has published two books for boys — Savage Gold and With My Little Eye — and four collections of verse: Poems (1939), The Middle of a War (1942), A Lost Season (1944) and Epitaphs and Occasions (1949). The two poems given here are from his second book.

Roy Fuller was a contributor to New Verse and to Twentieth Century Verse (edited by Julian Symons) in the 'thirties, and his verse echoes faithfully the social mood of that decade as — say — the verse of John Heath-Stubbs does the neo-romanticism of the 'forties. When neo-romanticism goes bad, it dissolves into a nasty pool of feeling in which swim faint, evocative fishes; when the social poetry of the 'thirties went bad, it was dull, prosy, as powder-dry as a country lane in a heat-wave. Roy Fuller generally avoids these faults. Auden taught him to observe and to arrange his observations in support of a particular interpretation of social reality. The war gave him more to observe and made him a better poet.

Poem

Reading the shorthand on a barber's sheet
In a warm and chromium basement in Cannon Street
I discovered again the message of the city,
That without power there is no place for pity.

The barber with a flat and scented hand
Moved the dummy's head in its collar band.
'What will you do with the discarded hair?'

The mirror showed a John the Baptist's face,
Detached and sideways. 'Can you tell me how,'
It said 'I may recover grace?'

'Make me a merchant, make me a manager.'
His scissors mournfully declined the task.
'Will you do nothing that I ask?'

'It is no use,' he said, 'I cannot speak
To you as one in a similar position.
For me you are the stern employer,
Of wealth the accumulator.
I must ignore your singular disposition.'

He brushed my shoulders and under his practised touch
I knew his words were only a deceit.
'You spoke to me according to the rules
Laid down for dealing with madmen and with fools.'

'I do my best,' he said, 'my best is sufficient.
If I have offended it is because
I never formulate the ideal action
Which depends on observation.'

'And do you never observe and never feel
Regret at the destruction of wealth by war?
Do you never sharpen your razor on your heel
And draw it across selected throats?'

He smiled and turned away to the row of coats.
'This is your mackintosh,' he said, 'you had no hat.
Turn left for the station and remember the barber.
There is just time enough for that.'

Harbour Ferry

The oldest and simplest thoughts
Rise with the antique moon:
How she enamels men
And artillery under her sphere,
Eyelids and hair and throats
Rigid in love and war;
How this has happened before.

And how the lonely man
Raises his head and shudders
With a brilliant sense of the madness,
The age and shape of his planet,
Wherever his human hand
Whatever his set of tenets,
The long and crucial minute.

To-night the moon has risen
Over a quiet harbour,
Through twisted iron and labour,
Lighting the half-drowned ships.
Oh surely the fatal chasm
Is closer, the furious steps
Swifter? The silver drips

From the angle of the wake:
The moon is flooding the faces.
The moment is over: the forces
Controlling lion nature
Look out of the eyes and speak:
Can you believe in a future
Left only to rock and creature?

GEORGE BARKER

*George Barker was born in Essex in 1913 and educated at an
L.C.C. School and the Regent Street Polytechnic. He taught
English Literature for a short time before the war in Japan and he
has also travelled in America. His first book of poems was published
when he was twenty. He followed this up with* Poems *(1935),*
Calamiterror *(1937),* Lament and Triumph *(1940) and* Eros in
Dogma *(1944). Two prose books are* Alanna Autumnal *and* Janus.

*Edwin Muir described Barker in 1939 as 'a poet of genius still at
the unformed stage', and* Calamiterror *as 'a pouring out of all sorts
of material, good and bad, deep and shallow'. There have been much
less favourable judgments. The truth, as I see it, is that few poets
can ever have written so well and so badly inside the covers of one
volume, sometimes inside a single poem. Reading his longer pieces
is therefore rather like riding a switchback, continually being jerked
and bucketed from some well-phrased perception into the bathetic
and the grotesque. Barker is still an unformed poet, and, in a sense,
his promise is still unfulfilled.*

*To characterize his work the reader needs to imagine a contention
between unequal elements of the visceral and the moral-didactic, or,
to put it another way, between a clumsier Dylan Thomas and a less
intelligent Spender. He was always more of a moralist-politician
than Dylan Thomas —*

> *... by being miserable for myself I began
> And now am miserable for the mass of man*

— and Calamiterror *was directly inspired by the Spanish Civil War:
and the didactic is on the whole his strength. See, for example,
'Allegory of the Adolescent and the Adult' and 'Resolution of
Dependence' in* Lament and Triumph, *his best book, from which
'Battersea Park' is reprinted. But even in this book he can write:*

> *Of James O'Hanlon who died at the hand
> Of the Black with Blood, the with sin Tan ...*

with an excruciating punning irrelevancy amounting to monumental bad taste. A similar absurdity disfigures 'Pacific Sonnets', which are often so fine, in Eros In Dogma. *For example, the last two lines of 'Sonnet X' read:*

> Renders it as wretched as the mistletoe minute
> To the statuesque Balderdash in it.

Yet 'To My Mother', from the same volume and reprinted here, seems to me a real achievement in the tender-comic, and the octet is perfectly written. George Barker, then, must be called a hit-or-miss artist, but, particularly in Lament and Triumph, *there are quite a number of hits.*

Battersea Park

Now it is November and mist wreathes the trees,
The horses cough their white blooms in the street,
Dogs shiver and boys run; the barges on the Thames
Lie like leviathans in the fog; and I meet
A world of lost wonders as I loiter in the haze
Where fog and sorrow cross my April days.

I recollect it was so often thus; with
Diamonds and pearls like mineral water pointing
The Park railings and the gardens' evergreens:
I spent my winters in summer's disappointments.
The things that burned so bright in my Augusts
Scattering me with their November dusts.

Now I marvel that I am again investigating
The fringes of the bare gardens in the winter.
I had expected to be otherwhere now,
Where the worm curls about the bone's splinter.
Now what good is the great world where I walk
That only revives desire to live once more?

How in the fog of failure and distress
Glitter of things seen in a flicker can
Paralyse will and deter determination,
Make a man afraid of the ghost of a man.
It is the wile of the world of crystal things
That catch the eye and keep me in their rings.

What I saw was Sorrow loitering along by
The Thames near the tall bridge by Battersea Park;
He had in his hand Pavlova or a swan,
And I heard him singly softly in the dark:
My twin, he sang to me, whatever of thine
Is sad and sorry, shall be glad of mine.

And he went on, singing a gay tune.
And now I know that the sorrow is this,
Not that the world a space of sorrow is
But that it's glad. O so gay a grief!
How can I ever be at home here
Where Sorrow sings of Joy in my ear?

How can I ever be happy here, where
The cock robin whistles with a gun at his breast;
Here where the flower has for bud a tear,
Here where Beauty breeds fodder for the Beast?
How can I here be happy when I know
I can be happy only here and now?

To My Mother

Most near, most dear, most loved and most far,
Under the window where I often found her
Sitting as huge as Asia, seismic with laughter,
Gin and chicken helpless in her Irish hand,
Irresistible as Rabelais, but most tender for
The lame dogs and hurt birds that surround her, –

She is a procession no one can follow after
But be like a little dog following a brass band.

She will not glance up at the bomber, or condescend
To drop her gin and scuttle to a cellar,
But lean on the mahogany table like a mountain
Whom only faith can move, and so I send
O all my faith and all my love to tell her
That she will move from mourning into morning.

LAWRENCE DURRELL

Lawrence Durrell was born in India in 1914 and lived there until he was sent home as a schoolboy to Canterbury. For several years after leaving school he led a bohemian life in London, at one time playing the piano in a nightclub for a living, at another working in a photographer's studio. Before the war he lived in Corfu — Prospero's Cell (*1946*) *is a book about it — and during the war he worked at the British Embassy in Cairo. In 1947 he was Press Representative at Rhodes, and at the present time he is living in the Argentine. He has written novels and edited magazines, but here I record only his collections of verse:* A Private Country (*1943*), Cities, Plains, and People (*1946*) *and* On Seeming to Presume (*1948*).

His work, in which the evocation of landscapes of the Aegean Islands and of the Near East plays an important part, has a sensuousness constantly kept in control by a witty, satirical temperament. I find this combination exhilarating and satisfying. His weaknesses are an occasional carelessness about making his meaning clear and a kind of undergraduate brashness. The poems chosen to represent him here are from A Private Country. *'The Death of General Uncebunke', a biography in little, consists of fourteen carols and five soliloquies with this preliminary note:*

Not satire but an exercise in ironic compassion, celebrating
a simplicity of heart which is proof against superiority or the
tooth of the dog ... After all, we may have had other criteria,
but they were only criteria.

I would have liked to print all fourteen carols and, lacking space,
ought perhaps to have chosen something else complete in itself. But
these poems please me, and I have used them on acquaintances as a
poetic intelligence test with results which seem to justify me. 'A
Ballad of the Good Lord Nelson' is good, not so clean, fun.

Three Carols

from

The Death of General Uncebunke

I

My uncle sleeps in the image of death.
In the greenhouse and in the potting-shed
The wrens junket: the old girl with the trowel
Is a pillar of salt, insufferably brittle.
His not to reason why, though a thinking man.
Beside his mesmeric incomprehension
The little mouse mopping and mowing,
The giraffe and the spin-turtle, these can
On my picture-book look insufferably little
But knowing, incredibly Knowing.

III

Aunt Prudence, she was the eye of the needle.
Sleeping, a shepherdess of ghostly sheep.
'Thy will be done in Baden Baden.
In Ouchy, Lord, and in Vichy.'
In the garden of the vicarage sorting stamps
Was given merit of the poor in spirit
For dusting a cinquefoil, tuning the little lamps.

Well, God sends weather, the English apple,
The weeping willow.
Grum lies the consort of Prudence quite:
Mum as a long fiddle in regimentals:
This sudden IT between two tropical thumbs.
Unwrinkle him, Lord, unriddle this strange gorgon,
For tall Prudence who softens the small lamps,
Gives humble air to the organ that it hums.

v

My uncle has gone beyond astronomy.
His sleep is of the Babylonian deep-sea
Darker than bitumen, defter than devil's alliances.
He has seen Golgotha in carnival:
Now in the shin-bone the smart worm
Presides at the death of the sciences,
The Trinity sleeps in his knee.

Curse Orion who pins my man like moth,
Who sleeps in the monotony of his zone,
Who is a daft ankle-bone among stars,
O shame on the beggar by silent lands
Who has nothing but carbon for his own.

Uncouple the flutes! Strike with the black rod!
Our song is no more plural, the bones
Are hollow without your air, Lord God.
Give us the language of diamonds or
The speech of the little stones.

A Ballad of the Good Lord Nelson

The Good Lord Nelson had a swollen gland,
Little of the scripture did he understand
Till a woman led him to the promised land
          Aboard the Victory, Victory O.

Adam and Evil and a bushel of figs
Meant nothing to Nelson who was keeping pigs,
Till a woman showed him the various rigs
    Aboard the Victory, Victory O.

His heart was softer than a new laid egg,
Too poor for loving and ashamed to beg,
Till Nelson was taken by the Dancing Leg
    Aboard the Victory, Victory O.

Now he up and did up his little tin trunk
And he took to the ocean on his English junk,
Turning like the hour-glass in his lonely bunk
    Aboard the Victory, Victory O.

The Frenchmen saw him a-coming there
With the one-piece eye and the valentine hair,
With the safety-pin sleeve and occupied air
    Aboard the Victory, Victory O.

Now you all remember the message he sent
As an answer to Hamilton's discontent –
There were questions asked about it in the Parliament
    Aboard the Victory, Victory O.

Now the blacker the berry, the thicker comes the juice.
Think of Good Lord Nelson and avoid self-abuse,
For the empty sleeve was no mere excuse
    Aboard the Victory, Victory O.

'England Expects' was the motto he gave
When he thought of little Emma out on Biscay's wave,
And remembered working on her like a galley-slave
    Aboard the Victory, Victory O.

The first Great Lord in our English land
To honour the Freudian command,
For a cast in the bush is worth two in the hand
   Aboard the Victory, Victory O.

Now the Frenchman shot him there as he stood
In the rage of battle in a silk-lined hood
And he heard the whistle of his own hot blood
   Aboard the Victory, Victory O.

Now stiff on a pillar with a phallic air
Nelson stylites in Trafalgar Square
Reminds the British what once they were
   Aboard the Victory, Victory O.

If they'd treat their women in the Nelson way
There'd be fewer frigid husbands every day
And many more heroes on the Bay of Biscay
   Aboard the Victory, Victory O.

DYLAN THOMAS

Dylan Thomas was born in 1914 at Swansea and educated at Swansea Grammar School. He spent a year as a newspaper reporter and followed this by reviewing and other journalistic jobs. Rejected for the army, he began to do B.B.C. and film work during the war, and he has made a reputation as a screen-writer, a writer for radio and a broadcaster. He has published the following books of verse: 18 Poems *(1934),* Twenty-Five Poems *(1936),* The Map of Love *(1939) – this collection is of prose and verse – and* Deaths and Entrances *(1946). His short stories and his semi-autobiographical* Portrait of the Artist as a Young Dog *may be mentioned among his other prose works.*

The poetry of Dylan Thomas has been widely acclaimed and with particular emphasis by Herbert Read ('... the most absolute poetry that has been written in our time ... '), Edith Sitwell ('A new poet has arisen who shows every sign of greatness. His work is on a huge scale both in theme and structurally') and Stephen Spender ('Dylan Thomas is a poet of whom, at times, we can use the word "genius" '). Geoffrey Grigson, who printed Thomas's early work in New Verse and recognized its promise, dissents from these judgments. He attacks Thomas for his neglect of a continuous line of meaning and for being, at times, fantastic and slovenly. There is, of course, a real disagreement here, but it is less than it at first sight appears. On the promise of Thomas's early poems there is agreement, but the rhetoric was too drunken, the insight too fragmentary, the lack of unity in most of the pieces too obvious, for his first two books to be spoken of as positive achievements. Certain poems did break through into real life before The Map of Love (1939), for example 'In Memory of Anne Jones' (reprinted there, first published in 1938), but much more frequent were poems like 'A Grief Ago', full of towering phrases and with a real structure, but arbitrarily obscure for lack of a central theme or any clear impulse on the poet's part beyond that of wishing to produce a poem. It is to be noted that Spender reserves his real praise of Dylan Thomas for the work produced after 1943 and collected in Deaths and Entrances (1946). It is also to be noted that the carping note in Mr Grigson's criticism is due not only to what he considers faults in Thomas's work, but to the use of Thomas as a spearhead in the attack on the kind of poetry written by Auden. It is a fact that Dylan Thomas fathered the Apocalyptic movement and with it a lot of bad thinking and bad writing, but the sins of the children should not always be visited on their fathers. Thomas has, in my opinion, moved in his later work towards the decorum of a more continuous 'narrative' of meaning, and both 'The Hunchback in the Park' and 'Poem in October' (reprinted here from Deaths and Entrances) are satisfactory in this respect.

For discussion of the poetry of Dylan Thomas the reader is referred to the critics mentioned above and to two articles: 'Dylan Thomas: A Pioneer' by Francis Scarfe in Auden and After; 'An

Approach to Dylan Thomas' by Linden Huddlestone *in* Penguin New Writing, No. 35.

A Grief Ago

A grief ago,
She who was who I hold, the fats and flower,
Or, water-lammed, from the scythe-sided thorn,
Hell wind and sea,
A stem cementing, wrestled up the tower,
Rose maid and male,
Or, masted venus, through the paddler's bowl
Sailed up the sun;

Who is my grief,
A chrysalis unwrinkling on the iron,
Wrenched by my fingerman, the leaden bud
Shot through the leaf,
Was who was folded on the rod the aaron
Rose cast to plague,
The horn and ball of water on the frog
Housed in the side.

And she who lies,
Like exodus a chapter from the garden,
Brand of the lily's anger on her ring,
Tugged through the days
Her ropes of heritage, the wars of pardon,
On field and sand
The twelve triangles of the cherub wind
Engraving going.

Who then is she,
She holding me? The people's sea drives on her,
Drives out the father from the caesared camp;

The dens of shape
Shape all her whelps with the long voice of water,
That she I have,
The country-handed grave boxed into love,
Rise before dark.

The night is near,
A nitric shape that leaps her, time and acid;
I tell her this: before the suncock cast
Her bone to fire.
Let her inhale her dead, through seed and solid
Draw in their seas,
So cross her hand with their grave gipsy eyes,
And close her fist.

In Memory of Ann Jones

After the funeral, mule praises, brays,
Windshake of sailshaped ears, muffle-toed tap
Tap happily of one peg in the thick
Grave's foot, blinds down the lids, the teeth in black,
The spittled eyes, the salt ponds in the sleeves,
Morning smack of the spade that wakes up sleep,
Shakes a desolate boy who slits his throat
In the dark of the coffin and sheds dry leaves,
That breaks one bone to light with a judgement clout,
After the feast of tear-stuffed time and thistles
In a room with a stuffed fox and a stale fern,
I stand, for this memorial's sake, alone
In the snivelling hours with dead, humped Ann
Whose hooded fountain heart once fell in puddles
Round the parched worlds of Wales and drowned each sun,
(Though this for her is a monstrous image blindly
Magnified out of praise; her death was a still drop;

H 2

She would not have me sinking in the holy
Flood of her heart's fame; she would lie dumb and deep
And need no druid of her broken body).
But I, Ann's bard on a raised hearth, call all
The seas to service that her wood-tongued virtue
Babble like a bellbuoy over the hymning heads,
Bow down the walls of the ferned and foxy woods
That her love sing and swing through a brown chapel,
Bless her bent spirit with four, crossing birds.
Her flesh was meek as milk, but this skyward statue
With the wild breast and blessed and giant skull
Is carved from her in a room with a wet window
In a fiercely mourning house in a crooked year.
I know her scrubbed and sour humble hands
Lie with religion in their cramp, her threadbare
Whisper in a damp word, her wits drilled hollow,
Her fist of a face died clenched on a round pain;
And sculptured Ann is seventy years of stone,
These cloud-sopped, marble hands, this monumental
Argument of the hewn voice, gesture and psalm
Storm me for ever over her grave until
The stuffed lung of the fox twitch and cry Love
And the strutting fern lay seeds on the black sill.

The Hunchback in the Park

The hunchback in the park
A solitary mister
Propped between trees and water
From the opening of the garden lock
That lets the trees and water enter
Until the Sunday sombre bell at dark

Eating bread from a newspaper
Drinking water from the chained cup
That the children filled with gravel

In the fountain basin where I sailed my ship
Slept at night in a dog kennel
But nobody chained him up.

Like the park birds he came early
Like the water he sat down
And Mister they called Hey mister
The truant boys from the town
Running when he had heard them clearly
On out of sound

Past lake and rockery
Laughing when he shook his paper
Hunchbacked in mockery
Through the loud zoo of the willow groves
Dodging the park keeper
With his stick that picked up leaves.

And the old dog sleeper
Alone between nurses and swans
While the boys among willows
Made the tigers jump out of their eyes
To roar on the rockery stones
And the groves were blue with sailors

Made all day until bell time
A woman figure without fault
Straight as a young elm
Straight and tall from his crooked bones
That she might stand in the night
After the locks and chains

All night in the unmade park
After the railings and shrubberies
The birds the grass the trees the lake

And the wild boys innocent as strawberries
Had followed the hunchback
To his kennel in the dark.

Poem in October

It was my thirtieth year to heaven
Woke to my hearing from harbour and neighbour wood
And the mussel pooled and the heron
        Priested shore
        The morning beckon
With water praying and call of seagull and rook
And the knock of sailing boats on the net webbed wall
        Myself to set foot
        That second
In the still sleeping town and set forth.

My birthday began with the water-
Birds and the birds of the winged trees flying my name
Above the farms and the white horses
        And I rose
        In rainy autumn
And walked abroad in a shower of all my days.
High tide and the heron dived when I took the road
        Over the border
        And the gates
Of the town closed as the town awoke.

A springful of larks in a rolling
Cloud and the roadside bushes brimming with whistling
Blackbirds and the sun of October
        Summery
        On the hill's shoulder,
Here were fond climates and sweet singers suddenly
Come in the morning where I wandered and listened

To the rain wringing
        Wind blow cold
In the wood faraway under me.

        Pale rain over the dwindling harbour
And over the sea wet church the size of a snail
        With its horns through mist and the castle
                Brown as owls
        But all the gardens
Of spring and summer were blooming in the tall tales
Beyond the border and under the lark full cloud.
        There could I marvel
                My birthday
Away but the weather turned around.

        It turned away from the blithe country
And down the other air and the blue altered sky
        Streamed again a wonder of summer
                With apples
        Pears and red currants
And I saw in the turning so clearly a child's
Forgotten mornings when he walked with his mother
        Through the parables
                Of sunlight
And the legends of the green chapels

        And the twice told fields of infancy
That his tears burned my cheeks and his heart moved in mine.
        These were the woods the river and sea
                Where a boy
                In the listening
Summertime of the dead whispered the truth of his joy
To the trees and the stones and the fish in the tide.
        And the mystery
                Sang alive
Still in the water and singingbirds.

And there could I marvel my birthday
Away but the weather turned around. And the true
Joy of the long dead child sang burning
In the sun.
It was my thirtieth
Year to heaven stood there then in the summer noon
Though the town below lay leaved with October blood.
O may my heart's truth
Still be sung
On this high hill in a year's turning.

NORMAN NICHOLSON

Norman Nicholson was born at Millom, Cumberland, in 1914. He has been a lecturer and tutor for the Workers' Educational Association in that county, and he has written a popular book on the subject of modern literature from a religious standpoint. His verse is built on two main elements – his Christianity and his understanding of his own region. In 1942 he edited An Anthology of Religious Verse *for* Pelican Books, *and his own first book of verse,* Five Rivers, *came out in 1944 – although his work had appeared earlier in magazines and in* Selected Poems, *a collection in which he was companioned by John Hall and Keith Douglas. His second book of poems,* Rock Face, *was issued in 1948. Between these he wrote the verse-play,* The Old Man of the Mountains, *performed in Martin Browne's 'season of new plays by poets' at the Mercury Theatre and published in 1946. The theme of the play is found in the story of Elijah and the raven, transferred to modern times and Nicholson's favourite Cumberland setting. His most recent books are a guide to Cumberland and a selection of Wordsworth's poems with a critical introduction. I have the feeling that he is an awkward poet to select from and that 'Poem for Epiphany' hardly does justice to his poetic individuality.*

Poem for Epiphany

Three Kings stepped out of my body,
Walked across the sand by the wild sea
From December into January.

A King stepped out of my head,
And before him the sand was red
And the sea gold,
And he beheld
The landscape like an empire and found in
Even a sycamore leaf the plan of his domain.
And he offered the gold of his sight
The regimen of his thought
To the Child born that night.

A King stepped out of my breast
Who had the bearing of a priest.
To him the moon's movement
Was a sacrament,
And the taste of water and of wine,
The touch of bread and the weight of a stone.
And he offered the frankincense of the heart,
Prayer swung in the censer on the charcoal alight,
To the Child born that night.

A King stepped out of my loins,
And black as grapes were his skin and his veins.
In him was the anger of sex
Where the blood like a sea on the shingle breaks,
The pride of living, the longing for further birth
Because of the presentiment of death.
And he offered the myrrh of tiredness, the untight'ning
    of the fingers from the nerve's root
To the Child born that night.

Three Kings stepped out of my body
But only my two eyes between the three —
Only my two eyes and the wild skies to see.

RUTHVEN TODD

*Ruthven Todd was born in Edinburgh in 1914 and educated at
Fettes and the Edinburgh College of Art, where he studied painting.
He put in two years as a farm labourer on the Isle of Mull before
coming to London in the mid-'thirties to pick up an existence tutor-
ing, selling pottery, and reviewing. Recently (1948) he has been
lecturing in the United States at Iowa, Chicago and elsewhere.
Between these dates he confesses that he has written a bewildering
number of books, including three novels, four volumes of verse and
two collections of essays – all of which are published or on the verge
of publication. He has also edited Gilchrist's* Life of Blake *for
Everyman's Library and Richard and Samuel Redgrave's* A Century of Painters of the English School *for the Phaidon Press.
To my knowledge even this list is incomplete, but out of it we may
select for mention by name the books of verse –* Until Now, The
Acreage of the Heart *and* The Planet in My Hand – *and the
interesting and original collection of essays,* Tracks in the Snow.
*Ruthven Todd's weakness as a writer has always been a dangerous
fluency and facility, but 'Personal History' represents the best level
of his verse, a level reached a number of times in his various books.*

Personal History

For my Son

O my heart is the unlucky heir of the ages,
And my body is unwillingly the secret agent
Of my ancestors; those content with their wages
From history: the Cumberland Quaker whose gentle
Face was framed with lank hair to hide the ears
Cropped as a punishment for his steadfast faith,
The Spanish lady who had seen the pitch lake's broth

In the West Indian island and the Fife farmers
To whom the felted barley meant a winter's want.

My face presents my history, and its sallow skin
Is parchment for the Edinburgh lawyer's deed:
To have and hold in trust, as feoffee therein
Until such date as the owner shall have need
Thereof. My brown eyes are jewels I cannot pawn,
And my long lip once curled beside an Irish bog,
My son's whorled ear was once my father's, then mine;
I am the map of a campaign, each ancestor has his flag
Marking an advance or a retreat. I am their seed.

As I write I look at the five fingers of my hand,
Each with its core of nacre bone, and rippled nails;
Turn to the palm and the traced unequal lines that end
In death – only at the tips my ancestry fails –
The dotted swirls are original and are my own:
Look at this fringed polyp which I daily use
And ask its history, ask to what grave abuse
It has been put: perhaps it curled about the stone
Of Cain. At least it has known much of evil,

And perhaps as much of good, been tender
When tenderness was needed, and been firm
On occasion, and in its past been free of gender,
Been the hand of a mother holding the warm
Impress of the child against her throbbing breast,
Been cool to the head inflamed in fever,
Sweet and direct in contact with a lover.
O in its cupped and fluted shell lies all the past,
My fingers close about the crash of history's storm.

In the tent of night I hear the voice of Calvin
Expending his hatred of the world in icy words;
Man less than a red ant beneath the towering mountain,
And God a troll more fearful than the feudal lords:

The Huguenots in me, flying St Bartholomew's Day,
Are in agreement with all this, and their resentful hate
Flames brighter than the candles on an altar, the grey
Afternoon is lit by catherine wheels of terror, the street
Drinks blood, and pity is death before their swords.

The cantilever of my bones acknowledges the architect,
My father, to whom always the world was a mystery
Concealed in the humped base of a bottle, one solid fact
To set against the curled pages and the tears of history.
I am a Border keep, a croft and a solicitor's office,
A country rectory, a farm and a drawing board:
In me, as in so many, the past has stowed its miser's hoard,
Won who knows where nor with what loaded dice.
When my blood pulses it is their blood I feel hurry.

These forged me, the latest link in a fertile chain
With ends that run so far that my short sight
Cannot follow them, nor can my weak memory claim
Acquaintance with the earliest shackle. In my height
And breadth I hold my history, and then my son
Holds my history in his small body and the history of another,
Who for me has no contact but that of flesh, his mother.
What I make now I make, indeed, from the unknown,
A blind man spinning furiously in the web of night.

HENRY REED

Henry Reed was born in Birmingham in 1914 and educated there. Having graduated M.A. of Birmingham University, where he was Charles Grant Robertson Scholar, he took to free-lance journalism, publishing articles chiefly on literature and travel in many papers, including the Birmingham Post *and* Manchester Guardian. *Later he did much reviewing, notably for the* New Statesman. *He is glad, he says, to have been in Birmingham 'one of a group of people which included Auden and MacNeice, John Hampson and Walter Allen, the painter John Melville, the critic Robert Melville and the sculptor Gordon Herrick'.*

He was called up in 1941, but was released from the army in 1942 and went to work at the Foreign Office. At the end of the war he returned to 'whole-time' writing. Since then he has done a good deal of broadcasting on books and films, and he has written success-ful radio scripts for the Third Programme such as Moby Dick *and* Pytheas. *The former of these has been published. A* Map of Verona *(1946), his only book of verse so far, has great competence in its varied manners and metres. 'Naming of Parts' and 'Judging Distances' appear in the section entitled 'Preludes' and are, I believe, among the best — as they are certainly among the most intelligent — poems produced during the war; but I would also have liked to include in this anthology, had space permitted, one of his less colloquial poems such as 'Philoctetes' or a section of the 'Tintagel' sequence. In these the influence of the later Eliot is inoffensively apparent. I should also have liked to print 'Chard Whitlow', the wickedest and funniest parody of Mr Eliot known to me.*

Lessons of the War

To Alan Michell

*Vixi duellis nuper idoneus
Et mlitavi non sine gloria*

I. Naming of Parts

To-day we have naming of parts. Yesterday,
We had daily cleaning. And to-morrow morning,
We shall have what to do after firing. But to-day,
To-day we have naming of parts. Japonica
Glistens like coral in all of the neighbouring gardens,
    And to-day we have naming of parts.

This is the lower sling swivel. And this
Is the upper sling swivel, whose use you will see,
When you are given your slings. And this is the piling swivel,
Which in your case you have not got. The branches
Hold in the gardens their silent, eloquent gestures,
    Which in our case we have not got.

This is the safety-catch, which is always released
With an easy flick of the thumb. And please do not let me
See anyone using his finger. You can do it quite easy
If you have any strength in your thumb. The blossoms
Are fragile and motionless, never letting anyone see
    Any of them using their finger.

And this you can see is the bolt. The purpose of this
Is to open the breech, as you see. We can slide it
Rapidly backwards and forwards: we call this
Easing the spring. And rapidly backwards and forwards
The early bees are assaulting and fumbling the flowers:
    They call it easing the Spring.

They call it easing the Spring: it is perfectly easy
If you have any strength in your thumb: like the bolt,
And the breech, and the cocking-piece, and the point of balance,
Which in our case we have not got; and the almond-blossom
Silent in all of the gardens and the bees going backwards and
        forwards,
    For to-day we have naming of parts.

II. *Judging Distances*

Not only how far away, but the way that you say it
Is very important. Perhaps you may never get
The knack of judging a distance, but at least you know
How to report on a landscape: the central sector,
The right of arc and that, which we had last Tuesday,
    And at least you know

That maps are of time, not place, so far as the army
Happens to be concerned -- the reason being,
Is one which need not delay us. Again, you know
There are three kinds of tree, three only, the fir and the poplar,
And those which have bushy tops to; and lastly
  That things only seem to be things.

A barn is not called a barn, to put it more plainly,
Or a field in the distance, where sheep may be safely grazing.
You must never be over-sure. You must say, when reporting:
At five o'clock in the central sector is a dozen
Of what appear to be animals; whatever you do,
  Don't call the bleeders *sheep*.

I am sure that's quite clear; and suppose, for the sake of example,
The one at the end, asleep, endeavours to tell us
What he sees over there to the west, and how far away,
After first having come to attention. There to the west,
On the fields of summer the sun and the shadows bestow
  Vestments of purple and gold.

The still white dwellings are like a mirage in the heat,
And under the swaying elms a man and a woman
Lie gently together. Which is, perhaps, only to say
That there is a row of houses to the left of arc,
And that under some poplars a pair of what appear to be humans
  Appear to be loving.

Well that, for an answer, is what we might rightly call
Moderately satisfactory only, the reason being,
Is that two things have been omitted, and those are important.
The human beings, now: in what direction are they,
And how far away, would you say? And do not forget
  There may be dead ground in between.

There may be dead ground in between; and I may not have got
The knack of judging a distance; I will only venture
A guess that perhaps between me and the apparent lovers,
(Who, incidentally, appear by now to have finished,)
At seven o'clock from the houses, is roughly a distance
      Of about one year and a half.

LAURIE LEE

Laurie Lee was born in 1914 in the Cotswolds. He spent some time wandering in Spain before the Civil War and his poems show that he has learnt something from Lorca. He was represented in Poets of Tomorrow, Third Selection *(1942), but his first complete volume was* The Sun My Monument *(1944). His second book of verse,* The Bloom of Candles, *is dated 1947. He has also written a documentary,* Land at War, *and two verse dramas:* Peasant's Priest, *performed at the Canterbury Festival; and* The Voyage of Magellan, *written for the B.B.C. Third Programme and since published.*

'April Rise' is printed from The Bloom of Candles, *which has the sub-title 'verses from a poet's year'. This second collection, which consists of only twelve poems, is at the same time less ambitious and from the viewpoint of craftsmanship a more finished job than* The Sun My Monument. *It accepts a narrower field and so avoids the clumsiness of such poems in the earlier book as 'Look into Wombs' and 'Port of Famagusta'. There is euphuism, I suggest, in Laurie Lee's combination of sophisticated recording of sensation with simple feeling, and perhaps a wilfulness in his romantic determination to avoid contemporaneity and achieve 'timeless' lyrics, but his best poems in* The Bloom of Candles — *'Christmas Landscape', 'Field of Autumn', 'April Rise' — have perhaps as much simplicity as Tennysonian simplesse.*

April Rise

If ever I saw blessing in the air
   I see it now in this still early day
Where lemon-green the vaporous morning drips
   Wet sunlight on the powder of my eye.

Blown bubble-film of blue, the sky wraps round
   Weeds of warm light whose every root and rod
Splutters with soapy green, and all the world
   Sweats with the bead of summer in its bud.

If ever I heard blessing it is there
   Where birds in trees that shoals and shadows are
Splash with their hidden wings and drops of sound
   Break on my ears their crests of throbbing air.

Pure in the haze the emerald sun dilates,
   The lips of sparrows milk the mossy stones,
While white as water by the lake a girl
   Swims her green hand among the gathered swans.

Now, as the almond burns its smoking wick,
   Dropping small flames to light the candled grass;
Now, as my low blood scales its second chance,
   If ever world were blessed, now it is.

PATRIC DICKINSON

Patric Dickinson was born on Boxing Day, 1914. He got his Blue for golf at Cambridge where he was an exhibitioner of St Catherine's College. From January 1945 until early 1949 he was a very successful Poetry Editor for the B.B.C. Home Service, and only left this position on receiving an Atlantic Award for Literature. His first book of verse was The Seven Days of Jericho. *Better known are* Theseus and the Minotaur and Poems *(1946), the title-piece of which has been broadcast, and* Stone in the Midst and Poems *(1949). 'Mankind and Star' is from the latter collection.* Stone in the Midst, *a verse play, has been produced at the* Mercury Theatre.

Mankind and Star

Orion or Plough or Bear
Or embodied zodiac
Relate mankind and star,
And of the Infinite make
A tolerable scale
For our imagination –
Create a constellation
Mundane or mythical.

O stars that are worn and spare
And long in coming back,
– Like soldiers from a war
For some forgotten sake
Who still must spin a tale
About the desolation –
Create a constellation
For those that flared and fell:

O shine upon us where
We lie linked in the dark —
(And none but I to share
Her light the heavens lack
To reaffirm the whole
Enigma of creation)
Create a constellation
Our own lives to foretell.

ALAN HODGE

Alan Hodge was born in Scarborough in 1915 and educated at Liverpool Collegiate School and Oriel College, Oxford. For a time before the war he worked with Robert Graves and Laura Riding, and poetry and prose by him appeared in Epilogue, *a critical miscellany issued by the Seizin Press, Majorca. During the war he was engaged at the Ministry of Information and he is now the general editor of a series of reprints of novels for a London publisher and also a financial journalist. He is married to a daughter of the American poet, Conrad Aiken.*

'The World of Nowhere' was printed in Work in Hand *(1942), a collection of poems by Robert Graves, Norman Cameron and Alan Hodge. He has also written two books of prose with Robert Graves:* The Long Week-End *(1940); and* The Reader Over Your Shoulder *(1943).*

The World of Nowhere

No matter where you start,
This world remains a place apart —
Nothing to find here after your own heart.

Everywhere your foreign eye,
Your foreign ear, no matter how they try
Catch no familiar gestures in reply.

The people here pursue,
Even if it is miracles you do,
A close serenity that puzzles you.

As for the countryside,
So many trees brush your glance aside,
Your greedy heart must go unsatisfied.

Only, perhaps, across an opening lake
Some travelled echo of the search you make
Will send you homeward for perfection's sake.

Be sure, this world of nowhere will expel
All who seek here a chance outlandish spell
That any place could offer just as well.

ALUN LEWIS

*Alun Lewis, who was born in 1915, came from a mining area of
South Wales. He read mediaeval history at an English provincial
university and took his M.A. degree in 1939. Having joined the
army, he went out to India in 1942 as a lieutenant in The South
Wales Borderers. Something of his physical existence there and
more of his mental life and of the things which were important to
him (his marriage, his Welsh descent – 'I know more Urdu than
Welsh: it's very sad', his ambitions for future stories and poems)
can be learnt from* Letters from India (1946), *selected by Gweno
Lewis and Gwyn Jones with a brief preface by A. L. Rowse. He
was killed in an accident in Arakan early in 1944.*

'Thinking back on my own writing', he had said in June 1943,

'it all seemed to mature of a sudden between the winter of 1939 and the following autumn. Can't make it out. Was it Gweno [his wife] and the Army? What a combination!!! Beauty and the Beast! His first collection of poems, Raiders' Dawn, containing the much-quoted 'All Day it has Rained' and revelatory of his devotion to Edward Thomas, came out in 1942 and was well received, as was The Last Inspection, a book of short stories. His second book of poems, Ha! Ha! among the Trumpets, appeared posthumously in 1944 with a foreword by Robert Graves, who had read the manuscript at the poet's request and advised on the revision and exclusion of certain poems.

The name of Alun Lewis has often been bracketed with that of Sidney Keyes when critics and columnists have discussed the best poets thrown up by the war, but it is possible that Lewis, had he lived, would have developed rather as a prose-writer than as a poet, and that his gift was only temporarily sharpened into poetic expression by war, love and separation. In all his writing there is a most attractive honesty and unpretentiousness – 'My longing', he said, 'is more and more for one thing only, integrity, and I discount the other qualities in people far too ruthlessly if they lack that fundamental sincerity and wholeness.' 'The Mahratta Ghats', which comes from the third part of Ha! Ha! among the Trumpets, has the directness and solidity which are to me the most positive of his qualities as a poet.

The Mahratta Ghats

The valleys crack and burn, the exhausted plains
Sink their black teeth into the horny veins
Straggling the hills' red thighs, the bleating goats
– Dry bents and bitter thistles in their throats –
Thread the loose rocks by immemorial tracks.
Dark peasants drag the sun upon their backs.

High on the ghat the new turned soil is red,
The sun has ground it to the finest red,

It lies like gold within each horny hand.
Siva has spilt his seed upon this land.

Will she who burns and withers on the plain
Leave, ere too late, her scraggy herds of pain,
The cow-dung fire and the trembling beasts,
The little wicked gods, the grinning priests,
And climb, before a thousand years have fled,
High as the eagle to her mountain bed
Whose soil is fine as flour and blood-red?
But no! She cannot move. Each arid patch
Owns the lean folk who plough and scythe and thatch
Its grudging yield and scratch its stubborn stones.
The small gods suck the marrow from their bones.

Who is it climbs the summit of the road?
Only the beggar bumming his dark load.
Who was it cried to see the falling star?
Only the landless soldier lost in war.

And did a thousand years go by in vain?
And does another thousand start again?

DAVID GASCOYNE

*David Gascoyne was born in 1916 and educated at Salisbury
Cathedral Choir School and the Regent Street Polytechnic. He
began to write early. His first book of poems was published when he
was sixteen and his first novel in the following year. He spent some
time in France, met certain surrealist poets and artists, and was
influenced to produce* A Short Survey of Surrealism *(1935) and a
volume of poems,* Man's Life Is This Meat *(1936). At this time he
also contributed many translations of Eluard, Aragon, Tzara, and
other French poets, to the literary magazines. Among other pre-war
publications may be mentioned* Holderlin's Madness *(1938), trans-*

*lations with prose and verse commentary. Later work, which began
to point in a new direction, appeared in* Poets of Tomorrow, Third
Selection *(1942); and his collection,* Poems 1937–42 *(1943), illustrated with drawings by Graham Sutherland, exemplifies the style
which has emerged from earlier experimentation. Perhaps I should
have written 'styles', for the book has several manners. It contains
translations from Jouve and Supervielle, a few poems written in
French, much work that in its freedom and boldness of imagery –
though not in its organization – still recalls his surrealist verse, and
a section of religious poems, which have been much praised, entitled
'Miserere'. The best of these in my opinion are 'Pieta' and 'Lachry-
mae', but in most of them there is a sense of strain, not apparent in
'A Wartime Dawn' by which he is represented here. The quality of
the 'reporting' in this poem seems to me to be very fine.*

A Wartime Dawn

Dulled by the slow glare of the yellow bulb;
As far from sleep still as at any hour
Since distant midnight; with a hollow skull
In which white vapours seem to reel
Among limp muddles of old thought; till eyes
Collapse into themselves like clams in mud ...
Hand paws the wall to reach the chilly switch;
Then nerve-shot darkness gradually shakes
Throughout the room. *Lie still* ... Limbs twitch;
Relapse to immobility's faint ache. And time
A while relaxes; space turns wholly black.

But deep in the velvet crater of the ear
A chip of sound abruptly irritates.
A second, a third chirp; and then another far
Emphatic trill and chirrup shrills in answer; notes
From all directions round pluck at the strings
Of hearing with frail finely-sharpened claws.
And in an instant, every wakened bird

Across surrounding miles of air
Outside, is sowing like a scintillating sand
Its throat's incessantly replenished store
Of tuneless singsong, timeless, aimless, blind.

Draw now with prickling hand the curtains back;
Unpin the blackout-cloth; let in
Grim crack-of-dawn's first glimmer through the glass.
All's yet half sunk in Yesterday's stale death,
Obscurely still beneath a moist-tinged blank
Sky like the inside of a deaf mute's mouth ...
Nearest within the window's sight, ash-pale
Against a cinder coloured wall, the white
Pearblossom hovers like a stare; rain-wet
The further housetops weakly shine; and there,
Beyond, hangs flaccidly a lone barrage-balloon.

An incommunicable desolation weighs
Like depths of stagnant water on this break of day. –
Long meditation without thought. – Until a breeze
From some pure Nowhere straying, stirs
A pang of poignant odour from the earth, an unheard sigh
Pregnant with sap's sweet tang and raw soil's fine
Aroma, smell of stone, and acrid breath
Of gravel puddles. While the brooding green
Of nearby gardens' grass and trees, and quiet flat
Blue leaves, the distant lilac mirages, are made
Clear by increasing daylight, and intensified.

Now head sinks into pillows in retreat
Before this morning's hovering advance;
(Behind loose lids, in sleep's warm porch, half hears
White hollow clink of bottles, – dragging crunch
Of milk-cart wheels, – and presently a snatch
Of windy whistling as the newsboy's bike winds near,
Distributing to neighbour's peaceful steps
Reports of last-night's battles); at last sleeps.

While early guns on Norway's bitter coast
Where faceless troops are landing, renew fire:
And one more day of War starts everywhere.

TERENCE TILLER

Terence Tiller was born in Cornwall in 1916 and educated in London and at Jesus College, Cambridge. He was awarded the Chancellor's Medal for English Verse in 1936 and lectured in history at Cambridge between 1937 and 1939. From 1939 until 1946 he was living in Egypt, where he had the position of Lecturer in English at the Fuad I University, Cairo, wrote literary journalism, gave talks to troops and did cipher work for G.H.Q., Middle East. On his return to England he worked for a short time with Patric Dickinson on verse programmes for the B.B.C. He has published the following books of poems: Poems *(1941);* The Inward Animal *(1943);* Unarm Eros *(1948). 'Egyptian Beggar' is from his last volume.*

Egyptian Beggar

Old as a coat on a chair; and his crushed hand,
as unexpressive as a bird's face, held
out like an offering, symbol of the blind,
he gropes our noise for charity. You could build
his long-deserted face up out of sand,
    or bear his weakness as a child.

Shuffling the seconds of a drugged watch, he
attends no answer to his rote; for soul's
and body's terrible humility,

stripped year by year a little barer, wills
nothing: he claims no selfhood in his cry:
    his body is an age that feels.

As if a mask, a tattered blanket, should
live for a little before falling, when
the body leaves it: so briefly in his dead
feathers of rags, and rags of body, and in
his crumpled mind, the awful and afraid
    stirs and pretends to be a man.

Earth's degradation and the voice of earth;
colour of earth and clothed in it; his eyes
white pebbles blind with deserts; the long growth
of landscape in his body: as if these
or these dead acres horribly gave birth:
    here will fall from him like disguise.

Only a sad and humble motion keeps
the little space he is, himself: to row
his mindless caves with ritual hand and lips,
and wonder dimly at his guilt: with no
memory of it now: it was perhaps
    too fearful, or too long ago.

JOHN HEATH-STUBBS

John Heath-Stubbs was born in London in 1918. He went to Queen's College, Oxford, where he met and became the friend of Sidney Keyes, whose work he influenced (see the notice on Keyes). He has published the following volumes of poems: Wounded Thammuz (1942), Beauty and the Beast (1944), The Divided Ways (1947), Poems from Giacomo Leopardi (1947). He has also edited Selected Poems of Jonathan Swift (*1948*) *and has written for various periodicals on Augustan, Romantic and modern poetry.*

John Heath-Stubbs can be called a neo-romantic with propriety, although he would doubtless — as Keyes did — disclaim attachment to the 'new and overwrought romanticism' which began early in the 'forties to replace in the little magazines the 'social' poetry of the 'thirties. 'The Divided Ways' seems to me one of his more disciplined poems. The influence of Edith Sitwell is noticeable.

The Divided Ways

In memory of Sidney Keyes

He has gone down into the dark cellar
To talk with the bright-faced Spirit with silver hair;
But I shall never know what word was spoken there.

.   .   .   .

My friend is out of earshot; our ways divided
Before we even knew we had missed each other.
For he advanced
Into a stony wilderness of the heart,
Under a hostile and a red-clawed Sun;
All that dry day, until the darkness fell,
I heard him going, and shouting among the canyons.
But I, struck backward from the Eastern Gate,
Had turned aside, obscure,
Beneath the unfriendly silence of the Moon,
My long white fingers on a small carved lute.
There was a forest, and faces known in childhood
Rose unexpected from the mirrored pools;
The trees had hands to clutch my velvet shoulders,
And birds of fever sang among the branches;
Till the dark vine-boughs, breaking as I seized them,
And dripping blood, cried out with my own voice:

'I also have known thirst, and the wanderer's terror! ...'
But I had lost my friend and the mountain paths.
And if there might have been another meeting –
The new Sun rising in a different sky,
Having repaired his light in the streams of Ocean,
And the Moon, white and maternal, going down
Over the virgin hills – it is too late
Ever to find it now.

And though it was in May that the reptile guns
And breeze-fly bullets took my friend away,
It is no time to forge a delicate idyll
Of the young shepherd, stricken, prone among
The flowers of Spring, heavy with morning dew,
And emblematic blood of dying gods :
Or that head pillowed on a wave's white fleece,
Softly drowning in a Celtic sea.
This was more harsh and meaningless than Winter.

But now, at last, I dare avow my terror
Of the pale vampire by the cooling grate;
The enemy face that doubled every loved one;
My secret fear of him and his cold heroes;
The meaning of the dream
Which was so fraught with trouble for us both;
And how, through this long autumn
(Sick and tempestuous with another sorrow)
His spirit, vexed, fluttered among my thoughts,
A bird returning to the darkened window –
The hard-eyed albatross with scissor bill.
And I would ask his pardon for this weakness.

But he is gone where no hallooing voice
Or beckoning hand may ever call him back;
And what is ours of him
Must speak impartially for all the world.
There is no personal word remains for me,

And I pretend to find no meaning here.
Though I might guess that other Singer's wisdom
Who saw in Death a dark immaculate flower
And tenderness in every falling Autumn,
This abstract music will not bring again
My friend to his warm room.
Inscrutable the darkness covers him.

SIDNEY KEYES

Sidney Keyes was born at Dartford, Kent, in May 1922, and educated at Dartford Grammar School, Tonbridge School and Oxford. He was commissioned in the Queen's Own Royal West Kent Regiment in September 1942, left England in the following March, and died during the last days of the Tunisian campaign in April 1943 after only a fortnight's active service. The Iron Laurel, *his first book of poems, was published in 1942 and his second volume,* The Cruel Solstice, *in 1944. In the same year he was posthumously awarded the Hawthornden Prize. His* Collected Poems, *edited by Michael Meyer in 1945, contain a valuable memoir with quotations from letters by Keyes expressing some of his ideas about poetry and about the death-wish, which is a recurrent theme in all his work.* Minos of Crete, *plays and stories with selections from the notebooks and a few early poems, was edited by Michael Meyer and appeared in 1948.*

Sidney Keyes, who was not twenty-one when he died, was considered by general critical consent at the time the most promising of the younger war-poets, and a re-reading of his poems – in spite of the presence of much that is naturally fragmentary and imitative – confirms this judgment. Of living writers, he wrote during the war, he accepted 'Eliot, Charles Williams, Graves (to some extent), my great friend John Heath-Stubbs.' Like Heath-Stubbs he may be labelled a neo-romantic – he has certain affiliations even with the

Apocalyptic group, but he seems to me to have had more poetic ability than any of its actual members. The most important poets of the last hundred years to him were Yeats and Rilke.

The three poems given here date from the autumn of 1941 before the writing of 'The Foreign Gate', a poem which was in Meyer's words 'the great turning-point in his life'. 'I feel myself rather isolated as a writer', he declared, and again 'I am not a man but a voice'. Something of this isolation and necessary loneliness is expressed in 'The Bards'. 'William Wordsworth' was suggested by the death-mask of the poet reproduced as a frontispiece in Herbert Read's study of Wordsworth. 'Death and the Lovers', originally called 'Dialogue at a Window' in an earlier version with a different ending, is one of a sequence of four poems, four 'postures' of death, but its separate publication here may be justified. The four poems were written in isolation and assembled only as a sequence later.

The Bards

Now it is time to remember the winter festivals
Of the old world, and see their raftered halls
Hung with hard holly; tongues' confusion; slow
Beat of the heated blood in those great palaces
Decked with the pale and sickled mistletoe;
And voices dying when the blind bard rises
Robed in his servitude, and the high harp
Of sorrow sounding, stills those upturned faces.

O it is such long learning, loneliness
And dark despite to master
The bard's blind craft; in bitterness
Of heart to strike the strings and muster
The shards of pain to harmony, not sharp
With anger to insult the merry guest.
O it is glory for the old man singing
Dead valour and his own days coldly cursed.

How ten men fell by one heroic sword
And of fierce foray by the unwatched ford,
Sing, blinded face; quick hands in darkness groping
Pluck the sad harp; sad heart forever hoping
Valhalla may be songless, enter
The moment of your glory, out of clamour
Moulding your vision to such harmony
That drunken heroes cannot choose but honour
Your stubborn blinded pride, your inward winter.

William Wordsworth

No room for mourning: he's gone out
Into the noisy glen, or stands between the stones
Of the gaunt ridge, or you'll hear his shout
Rolling among the screes, he being a boy again.
He'll never fail nor die
And if they laid his bones
In the wet vaults or iron sarcophagi
Of fame, he'd rise at the first summer rain
And stride across the hills to seek
His rest among the broken lands and clouds.
He was a stormy day, a granite peak
Spearing the sky; and look, about its base
Words flower like crocuses in the hanging woods,
Blank though the dalehead and the bony face.

From Four Postures of Death

II Death and the Lovers

THE LOVER. The briars fumble with the moon;
    Far have I come, O far away
    And heartsick sore, my own sweeting.

THE WOMAN. I stand before the ordered prison room.
I can give you no lover's greeting.

THE LOVER. Wind cracks the clouds, so has my face cracked
open.
With longing all this while my cold face turning
Hopelessly to you, like a hound's blind muzzle
Turned to the moon.

THE WOMAN. O you bring in a sickly moon
And you bring in the rain:
I will not open, my true love is gone,
You are his ghost. O never come again.

THE LOVER. My feet are bleeding, you called me and your
face
Called me a daylong dreary journeying.

THE WOMAN. Get back, get back into your likely place.
The time is past for all this havering.

THE LOVER. I am a poor boy, pity
A poor boy on the roads, after your love.

THE WOMAN. It is too late: seek out a storied city
To house your silliness. Oh, my lost love ...

DEATH. Is here behind you. Get you in
Out of that muscular salacious wind.
Lie down by me: I have an art
To comfort you and still your restless mind.

THE WOMAN. I'll close the window; and God send
We are damned easily ...

DEATH. Lie down by me, be gentle: at the end
Of time, God's quiet hands will kill your
fantasy.

THE LOVER.   And strangle me, God's horny fingers, huge
             Fingers of broken cloud, great creaking hands
             That so beset me; briar-nails tear free
             My soul into your wisdom, ravish me
             Since she will not ...

THE WOMAN.   I am afraid, your hands are strong and cold.
             Are you my enemy, or my forsaken lover?

DEATH.   Lie soft, lie still. I am sleep's cruel brother.

Acknowledgments

For permission to reprint copyright matter, the following acknowledgments are made:

For poems by W. B. Yeats, to Mrs Yeats and Messrs Macmillan & Co.

> *Collected Poems* (Macmillan).
> *Last Poems* (Macmillan).

For the poem by Laurence Binyon, to the Society of Authors and Messrs Macmillan & Co.

> *The Burning of the Leaves* (Macmillan).

For poems by Walter de la Mare, to the author and Messrs Faber and Faber.

> *Collected Poems* (Faber).
> *The Burning Glass* (Faber).

For poems by Edward Thomas, to Mrs Thomas and Messrs Faber and Faber.

> *Collected Poems* (Faber).

For the poem by Harold Monro, to Mrs Alida Monro and the Poetry Bookshop, Messrs Cobden-Sanderson and Messrs John Lane (The Bodley Head).

> *Collected Poems* (Cobden-Sanderson).

For the poem by James Joyce, to his literary executors and Messrs Faber and Faber.

> *Finnegan's Wake* (Faber).

For poems by Wyndham Lewis, to the author and Messrs Faber and Faber.

> *One-Way Song* (Faber).

12

For poems by D. H. Lawrence, to Mrs Frieda Lawrence and Messrs William Heinemann.

> *Collected Poems* (Secker).
> *Last Poems* (Secker).

For the poem by Andrew Young, to the author and Messrs Jonathan Cape.

> *Speak to the Earth* (Cape).

For the poem by Charles Williams, to his literary executors and the Oxford University Press.

> *Taliessin Through Logres* (O.U.P.).

For poems by Siegfried Sassoon, to the author and Messrs Faber and Faber.

> *Collected Poems* (Faber).

For poems by Edwin Muir, to the author and Messrs Faber and Faber.

> *The Narrow Place* (Faber).
> 'The Combat' is uncollected, but has appeared in *The Listener*.

For poems by T. S. Eliot, to the author and Messrs Faber and Faber.

> *Collected Poems 1909–1935* (Faber).
> *Murder in the Cathedral* (Faber).
> *The Family Reunion* (Faber).

For poems by Arthur Waley, to the author and Messrs George Allen and Unwin.

> *Chinese Poems* (Allen and Unwin).

For the poem by Isaac Rosenberg, to Mrs I. Wynick and Messrs Chatto and Windus.

> *Collected Works* (Chatto and Windus).

For the poem by Richard Church, to the author and Messrs J. M. Dent & Sons.

The Lamp (Dent).

For the poem by Herbert Read, to the author and Messrs Faber and Faber.

Collected Poems (Faber).

For poems by Wilfred Owen, to his literary executors and Messrs Chatto and Windus.

Poems (Chatto and Windus).

For poems by Aldous Huxley, to the author and Messrs Chatto and Windus.

Leda (Chatto and Windus).

For poems by Robert Graves, to the author and Messrs Cassell & Co.

Collected Poems 1914–1947 (Cassell).

For poems by Edmund Blunden, to the author and Messrs Macmillan & Co.

Poems 1914–1930 (Macmillan).
Shells by a Stream (Macmillan).

For poems by Sacheverell Sitwell, to the author and Messrs Faber and Faber.

Canons of Giant Art (Faber).

For poems by Roy Campbell, to the author and Messrs Faber and Faber.

Sons of the Mistral (Faber).

For the poem by Michael Roberts, to Mrs Roberts and Messrs Faber and Faber.

Orion Marches (Faber).

For poems by William Plomer, to the author and Messrs Jonathan Cape.

The Dorking Thigh (Cape).

For poems by Cecil Day Lewis, to the author, the Hogarth Press and Messrs Jonathan Cape.

    Collected Poems (Hogarth Press).
    Overtures to Death (Cape).
    Word Over All (Cape).
    Poems 1943–1947 (Cape).

For the poem by Peter Quennell, to the author and Messrs Chatto and Windus.

    Poems (Chatto and Windus).

For the poem by Rex Warner, to the author and Messrs John Lane (The Bodley Head).

    Poems (Boriswood).

For poems by Norman Cameron, to the author, Messrs J. M. Dent & Sons and the Hogarth Press.

    The Winter House (Dent).
    Work in Hand (Hogarth Press).

For the poem by Vernon Watkins, to the author and Messrs Faber and Faber.

    The Lamp and the Veil (Faber).

For poems by John Betjeman, to the author and Messrs John Murray.

    Continual Dew (John Murray).
    New Bats in Old Belfries (John Murray).

For poems by William Empson, to the author and Messrs Faber and Faber.

    The Gathering Storm (Faber).

For poems by Louis MacNeice, to the author and Messrs Faber and Faber.

    Poems (Faber).
    The Earth Compels (Faber).
    Plant and Phantom (Faber).
    Springboard (Faber).

For poems by W. H. Auden, to the author and Messrs Faber and Faber.

> *The Dog Beneath the Skin* (Faber).
> *Another Time* (Faber).
> *Journey to a War* (Faber).
> *New Year Letter* (Faber).
> *For the Time Being* (Faber).

For the poem by John Lehmann, to the author and the Hogarth Press.

> *The Sphere of Glass* (Hogarth Press).

For poems by Kathleen Raine, to the author and Messrs Nicholson and Watson (P.L. Editions).

> *Stone and Flower* (Editions Poetry, London).
> *Living in Time* (Editions Poetry, London).

For poems by Stephen Spender, to the author and Messrs Faber and Faber.

> *Poems* (Faber).
> *The Still Centre* (Faber).
> *Ruins and Visions* (Faber).
> *Poems of Dedication* (Faber).

For poems by W. R. Rodgers, to the author and Messrs Secker and Warburg.

> *Awake! and Other Poems* (Secker and Warburg).

For poems by Bernard Spencer, to the author and Messrs Nicholson and Watson (P.L. Editions).

> *Aegean Islands* (Editions Poetry, London).
> 'On the Road' is uncollected, but has appeared in *Penguin New Writing*.

For the poem by Rayner Heppenstall, to the author and Messrs Secker and Warburg.

> *Poems 1933–1945* (Secker and Warburg).

For the poem by Francis Scarfe, to the author.

    'Tyne Dock' is uncollected, but has appeared in *The Listener*.

For poems by Charles Madge, to the author and Messrs. Faber and Faber.

    The Father Found (Faber).
    'Inscription I' has not previously been printed.

For the poem by Henry Treece, to the author and Messrs Faber and Faber.

    Invitation and Warning (Faber).

For poems by Anne Ridler, to the author and Messrs Faber and Faber.

    The Nine Bright Shiners (Faber).

For poems by Kenneth Allott, to the Cresset Press.

    The Ventriloquist's Doll (Cresset Press).

For the poem by F. T. Prince, to the author.

    'Soldiers Bathing' is uncollected, but first appeared in *Poems from the Forces*.

For poems by Roy Fuller, to the author and the Hogarth Press.

    The Middle of a War (Hogarth Press).

For poems by George Barker, to the author and Messrs Faber and Faber.

    Lament and Triumph (Faber).
    Eros in Dogma (Faber).

For poems by Lawrence Durrell, to the author and Messrs Faber and Faber.

    A Private Country (Faber).

For poems by Dylan Thomas, to the author and Messrs J. M. Dent & Sons.

Twenty-Five Poems (Dent).
The Map of Love (Dent).
Deaths and Entrances (Dent).

For the poem by Norman Nicholson, to the author and Messrs Faber and Faber.

Five Rivers (Faber).

For the poem by Ruthven Todd, to the author.

For poems by Henry Reed, to the author and Messrs Jonathan Cape.

The Map of Verona (Cape).

For the poem by Laurie Lee, to the author and Messrs John Lehmann.

The Bloom of Candles (Lehmann).

For the poem by Patric Dickinson, to the author and Messrs Methuen & Co.

Stone in the Midst and Poems (Methuen).

For the poem by Alan Hodge, to the author and the Hogarth Press.

Work in Hand (Hogarth Press).

For the poem by Alun Lewis, to his literary executors and Messrs. George Allen and Unwin.

Ha! Ha! among the Trumpets (Allen and Unwin).

For the poem by David Gascoyne, to the author and Messrs Nicholson and Watson (P.L. Editions).

Poems 1937–1942 (Editions Poetry, London).

For the poem by Terence Tiller, to the author and the Hogarth Press.

Unarm Eros (Hogarth Press).

For the poem by John Heath-Stubbs, to the author and Messrs Routledge & Kegan Paul Ltd.

The Divided Ways (Routledge).

For poems by Sidney Keyes, to his literary executors and Messrs Routledge & Kegan Paul Ltd.

Collected Poems (Routledge).

Index to First Lines

Drama

*

FOUR ENGLISH COMEDIES*

Edited by J. M. Morrell

763

The four plays in this volume have been chosen as representing the peaks of the tradition of English comedy between the Elizabethan age and its new flowering in modern times. All of them – Jonson's *Volpone*, Congreve's *Way of the World*, Goldsmith's *She Stoops to Conquer* and Sheridan's *School for Scandal* – have been revived in recent years with enormous success on the modern stage.

SALOME AND OTHER PLAYS

Oscar Wilde

600

Salome, with its odd moonlit beauty and the luxuriance of its language, is more akin to a modern prose poem than to drama proper. The other two plays in this volume – *A Woman of No Importance* and *An Ideal Husband* – are true Wildean comedies, presenting serious themes in an easy, witty and fast-moving style. Readers may remember the recent screen version of *An Ideal Husband*.

HASSAN

James Elroy Flecker

675

Based on some old Turkish tales, this is a play which was written when the author was working in the Middle East in 1911. It has proved one of the most spectacular plays to be seen on the modern English stage, and has been broadcast with equal success.

A SHORT HISTORY OF ENGLISH DRAMA

B. Ifor Evans

A 172

This author's *Short History of English Literature*, one of the most successful of Pelicans, is now followed by a similar survey of English Drama. It covers the whole development from the Middle Ages to modern times and will prove an indispensable guide to all students professional or otherwise.

*One shilling and sixpence each   * Two shillings and sixpence*

Literature and The Arts

*

A BOOK OF ENGLISH ESSAYS

Edited by W. E. Williams

A99

This selection includes such well-known essays as Charles Lamb's ' In Praise of Chimney Sweepers ' and de Quincey's ' On Knocking at the Gate in Macbeth ', and also many brilliant articles which have not often appeared in anthologies. Modern writers, moreover, such as Belloc, Priestley, Aldous Huxley, Robert Lynd and Ivor Brown are well represented.

THE MEANING OF ART*

Herbert Read

A213

Described in the *Star* when it first appeared as ' the best pocket introduction to the understanding of art that has ever been published ', this book is illustrated with sixty-six half tones and three line drawings. It has been newly revised for the Pelican series.

THE SYMPHONY*

Edited by Ralph Hill

A204

A guide which will assist the intelligent and serious listener towards a deeper understanding of those masterpieces of symphony which he is likely to hear frequently. The works of twenty composers are discussed by leading critics.

A SHORT HISTORY OF ENGLISH LITERATURE

B. Ifor Evans

A72

Covering the whole of English literature from Beowulf to James Joyce, a period of over a thousand years, and crowded with facts, this is a volume easy to read and full of original judgments. Commenting in *The Observer* on its leisurely movement combined with masterly compression, Ivor Brown described the book as written ' to the classical model, as brief as lucid '.

*One shilling and sixpence each   * Two shillings and sixpence*